ART AND ARCHITECTURE OF
THE INCAS

ART AND ARCHITECTURE OF
THE INCAS

An illustrated history of the arts, crafts and design of the first peoples
of South America, shown in 250 rich and vibrant photographs

David M Jones

southwater

This edition is published by Southwater
An imprint of Anness Publishing Ltd, Blaby Road,
Wigston, Leicestershire LE18 4SE

info@anness.com
www.southwaterbooks.com;
www.annesspublishing.com

Anness Publishing has a new picture agency outlet
for images for publishing, promotions or advertising.
Please visit our website www.practicalpictures.com
for more information.

Publisher: Joanna Lorenz
Editor: Joy Wotton
Designer: Nigel Partridge
Illustrations and maps: Vanessa Card and
  Anthony Duke
Production Controller: Steve Lang

ETHICAL TRADING POLICY
Because of our ongoing ecological investment programme,
you, as our customer, can have the pleasure and
reassurance of knowing that a tree is being cultivated
on your behalf to naturally replace the materials used to
make the book you are holding. For further information
about this scheme, go to www.annesspublishing.com/trees

Previously published as part of a larger volume
The Everyday Life of the Ancient Incas

PUBLISHER'S NOTE
Although the information in this book is believed to
be accurate and true at the time of going to press,
neither the authors nor the publisher can accept any
legal responsibility or liability for any errors or
omissions that may have been made nor for any
inaccuracies nor for any loss, harm or injury that
comes about from following information in this book.

PICTURE CREDITS
The Art Archive: 36b, 37t, 69tl; /Gianni Dagli Orti:
16t, 20t, 21t and b; /Album/J.Enrique Molina: 41t;
/Amano Museum Lima/Mireille Vautier: 81t, 105b,
106t; /Archaeological Museum Lima/Gianni Dagli
Orti: 35t, 68t, 72b, 81b, 85b, 86t, 87t, 89t, 94t and b,
96t, 97t and b, 100t and br, 101b, 104t, 122b, 123t;
/Archaeological Museum Lima/Mireille Vautier: 40t
and b, 73b, 83t, 84b, 86b, 89b, 98t, 110b; /Brunning
Museum, Lambeyeque, Peru/Mireille Vautier: 116t;
/Central Bank Museum/Mireille Vautier: 78t; /Dagli Orti:
22br; /Daniele Lavallée Collection Paris/Gianni Dagli
Orti: 84t; /E. Poli Collection Lima/Gianni Dagli Orti:
76b, 83b, 85t; /Gianni Dagli Orti: 5.3, 9r, 24t and b, 26br,
27t, 30b, 31b, 33t, 37b, 42t, 43t, 54t, 55b, 60–1, 62t, 63t,
65t, 69tr, 70b, 71b; /Mireille Vautier: 43b, 80t; /Museo
Amano Lima: 78b; /Museo Banco Central de Quito
Ecuador/Gianni Dagli Orti: 80b, 113t, 123b; /Museo de
Arte Municipal Lima/Gianni Dagli Orti: 101t; /Museo
del Oro Bogota/Gianni Dagli Orti: 111bl; /Museo del Oro
Lima/Gianni Dagli Orti: 103t, 104b, 110t, 112b, 113b,
115t, 118b, 119b, 121b, 125b; /Museo Guayasamin
Quito Ecuador/Gianni Dagli Orti: 82; /Museo Larco
Herrera Lima: 111t; /Museo Nacional Tiahuanacu La
Paz Bolivia /Gianni Dagli Ort: 87b, 121t; /Museo
Regional de Ica Peru/Gianni Dagli Orti: 72t, 88t.
Andrew McLeod: 11r, 26t, 38b, 58t, 63b.
Corbis: /© Brian A. Vikander: 5.1; /Atlantide
Phototravel: 23t; /Brian A. Vikander: 12–12; /Brian A.
Vikander: 53b; /Charles and Josette Lenars: 64t and
b; /Francesco Venturi: 77b; /Richard List: 65b.
Frances Reynolds: 5tr, 7br, 9l and m, 11l and m, 26bl,
27bl and br, 42b, 126, 128b.
Sally Phillips: 92t, 127t.
South American Pictures: /Anna McVittie: 52b;
/Archaeological Museum Lima/Gianni Dagli Orti:
100t; /Bill Leimbach: 102b; /Britt Dyer: 22bl, 25t,
68b; /Chris Sharp: 48br, 76t, 100bl, 124t; /Gianni
Dagli Orti: 55b; /Kathy Jarvis: 34, 35b, 39t, 57bl;
/Kim Richardson: 52t; /Kimball Morrison: 25b, 96b;
/Philippe Bowles: 59b; /Robert Francis: 8, 17t, 18b,
22t, 48bl, 49b, 55t, 70t; /Tony Morrison: 5.2, 5.4, 6tl,
7tl and tr, 10l and m, 14b, 15t and b, 16b, 17b, 18t,
19b, 28–9, 30t, 32b, 33b, 38t, 39bl, 41b, 46t and b,
47t, 49t, 50b, 51t, 53t, 56t, 57br, 58b, 62b, 66t and b,
67t, 69b, 73t, 74–5, 78tl, tr and b, 99tr and b, 102t,
106b, 107t, 115b, 116b, 117b, 120t.
The Werner Forman Archive: /Art Institute of
Chicago: /British Museum, London: 92b; /Dallas
Museum of Art: 1, 5.5, 5.6, 90–1, 105t, 108–9, 119t,
124b; /David Bernstein Fine Art, New York: 95, 103b,
111br, 112t, 122t; /Museum fur Volkerkunde, Berlin:
107b, 117t, 120b; /N.J. Saunders: 10r, 31t, 32t, 36t,
45b, 47b, 48t, 50t, 51b, 56b, 71t, 98b, 114t; /Private
Collection: 88b, 114b; /Rassiga Collection: 93t;
Museum fur Volkerkunde, Berlin: 118t.

*p.1 Lambeyeque-Sicán gold burial mask. p.2 Machu
Picchu. p.3 Astrologer, from a drawing by Poma de
Ayala's* Neuva Corónica, *c.1615.*

CONTENTS

INTRODUCTION

The vast continent of South America, nearly separate geologically and geographically from North America, never formed a single cultural unit. Its inhabitants developed at different paces, although cultures in large areas were aware of and interactive with each other through trade, political alliance, conquest and the diffusion of ideas.

The ancient cultures that archaeologists call 'civilizations' (urban-based societies with centralized political organization and advanced technology) were confined to the Andes mountains and adjacent western coastal valleys and deserts. Sophisticated societies and beliefs were also developed by other South American peoples, but they did not build monumental ceremonial centres or cities, or, for the most part, develop technology of the same complexity or variety as Andean cultures, or establish kingdoms and empires.

This book concentrates on the 'Andean Area', where civilizations evolved in the sierras and adjacent foothills and coastal regions, north to south from the present-day Colombian–Ecuadorian border to the northern half of Chile and east to west from the Amazonian Rainforest to the Pacific.

CONTACT WITH OTHER SOCIETIES

The Andean Area is a nuclear region, or cluster of settlements surrounded by natural borders, where civilization emerged independently. Other nuclear regions include Mesopotamia, Egypt, north-west India, China, South-east Asia and Mesoamerica. Ancient Andeans had no direct knowledge of or contact with the peoples of any other regions. There is no substantiated confirmation in written records, or any unequivocal archaeological evidence, to prove that sustained contact existed between the Old World and the New before 1492. There is equally no evidence to suggest the Incas were aware of the Aztec Empire or Maya city-states in Mesoamerica.

Below: Totora-reed boats on Lake Titicaca. Design has changed little since ancient times.

Above: Inca farmers tending maize seedlings in irrigated fields , depicted in Poma de Ayala's Nueva Corónica, c.1615.

By the 1520s, Inca traders were travelling up the north-west coast, making contact and trading with sophisticated metallurgy-producing 'chiefdoms' in north-western South America. Likewise, in the early 16th century, Aztecs traded at the international emporium of Xicalango in the Yucatán Peninsula, and were on the verge of invading the Maya city-states. The two empires might eventually have met, and the consequences would undoubtedly have been interesting.

WHAT IS CIVILIZATION?

Civilization is an elusive term. Much has been written in an attempt to define it, to list its essential characteristics. Standard dictionary definitions help little, for they tend to state that civilization is the 'opposite of barbarism', and that it involves the arts and refinement of culture. The end product – cultures with cities and a high level of sophisticated technology – seems obvious. Civilization is recognizable when full-blown. But it is the point at which civilization can be said to arrive that is so difficult to perceive and define.

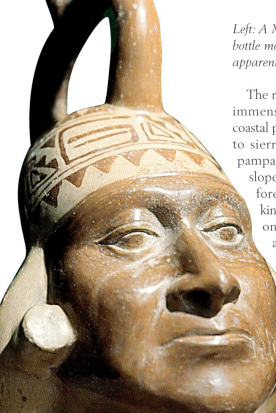

Left: A Moche stirrup-spout effigy bottle modelled as the head of an apparently blind man.

The range of contrasting landscapes was immense in the Andean Area – from coastal plains and deserts, to inland valleys, to sierra basins and plateaux, to high pampas grasslands, to eastern mountain slopes descending to Amazonian rainforests. Pre-Inca Andean city-states, kingdoms and empires evolved, based on maize and potato agriculture and on the herding of camelids (llamas, alpacas and vicuñas). Access to and control of water was a key factor in Andean cultural development and endurance, and this factor became important not only functionally, but also religiously.

Geographical contrast fostered and nurtured the development of sophisticated agriculture based on complex irrigation technologies and a wide variety of crops, both within and between lowland and highland regions. These developments fostered economic specialization, enabling cultures to develop social hierarchies and complex divisions and distributions of labour and rulership. Ancient Andeans developed trading contacts across long distances, and religious beliefs and structures, both theoretical and architectural.

LEGACY

As this book shows, the sophisticated technologies developed in Andean civilization came to be sponsored by the state. The growth of Ancient Andean cities, and their rulers and the religious hierarchy required large-scale production of exquisite ceramics, textiles and jewellery as statements of social status, state power and religious devotion. Sadly, these precious archaeological objects attract the

Above: Professor John Howland Rowe at the Palace of Emperor Huyana Capac, Peru. Archaeological evidence is our best source of information about everyday life.

interest and greed of modern collectors as much as they do scholars seeking the knowledge such objects can reveal. Since the Spanish Conquest, a legacy of illicit digging for monetary gain and exclusive ownership has fostered trade in antiquities fed by looting on a grand scale.

Undisturbed archaeological evidence, from the humblest building to the elite tombs of Sipán, provides the best source of information about everyday culture and conspicuous consumption of precious objects in their social and ritual contexts.

Below: An alpaca herd grazing in the highland Valle de Coloa, Bolivia. Pre-Inca Andean city states relied on the herding of camelids.

'Laundry lists' of criteria by which civilization can be defined have been made. They include: size, rulership, cities, domesticated animals and plants, irrigation agriculture, social organization (which includes individuals who do not participate in or contribute directly to subsistence), writing, a monetary system, a state army, a road system and a certain level of technological sophistication with specialized craftspeople. Yet every nuclear area listed above lacked one or more of these criteria.

ANDEAN CIVILIZATION

The Andean Area is vast. Within it, long-distance communication and exchange was a major feature of its civilization. Communication was long-lived, for as each successive culture developed, it was based on the developments that preceded it.

TIMELINE OF THE INCAS AND THEIR ANCESTORS

CHRONOLOGY OF ANDEAN AREA CIVILIZATION

The chronology of the Andean Area is complex. Archaeologists have developed a scheme based on technological achievements and on changing political organization through time, from the first arrival of humans in the area (15,000–3500BC) to the conquest of the Inca Empire by Francisco Pizarro in 1532. The pace of technological development varied in different regions within the Andean Area, especially in early periods in its history. The development of lasting and strong contact between regions, however, spread both technology and ideas and led to regions depending on each other to some degree. Sometimes this interdependence was due to large areas being under the control of one 'authority', while at other times the unifying link was religious or based on trade/technology.

The principal chronological scheme for the Andean Area comprises a sequence of eight time units: five Periods and three Horizons. Periods are defined as times when political unity across regions was less consolidated. Smaller areas were controlled by city-states, sometimes in loose groupings,

Above: The walled royal compounds of the Chimú capital Chan Chan.

perhaps sharing religious beliefs despite having different political views. The Horizons, by contrast, were times when much larger political units were formed. These units exercised political, economic and religious control over extended areas, usually including different types of terrain rather than being confined to coastal valley groups or sierra city-states.

Different scholars give various dates for the beginnings and endings of the Periods and Horizons, and no two books on Andean civilization give exactly the same dates. The durations of Periods and

Horizons also vary from one region to another within the Andean Area, and the charts have increased in complexity as authors have divided the Andean Area into coastal, sierra and Altiplano regions, or even into north, central and southern coastal regions and north, central and southern highland regions. The dates given here are a compilation from several sources, thus avoiding any anomalies in any specific sources.

CHRONOLOGICAL PERIOD	DATES	PRINCIPAL CULTURES
Lithic / Archaic Period	15,000–3500BC	spread of peoples into the Andean Area hunter-gatherer cultures
Preceramic / Formative Period (Cotton Preceramic)	3500–1800BC	early agriculture and first ceremonial centres
Initial Period	1800–750BC	U-shaped ceremonial centres, platform mounds and sunken courts
Early Horizon	750–200BC	Chavín, Paracas, Pukará (Yaya-Mama) cults
Early Intermediate Period	200BC–AD600	Moche, Nazca and Titicaca Basin confederacies
Middle Horizon	AD600–1000	Wari and Tiwanaku empires
Late Intermediate Period	AD1000–1400	Chimú and Inca empires
Late Horizon	AD1400–1532	Inca Empire and Spanish Conquest

LITHIC / ARCHAIC PERIOD (15,000–3500BC)

Above: View from the Cuz del Condor showing the mountains and valleys of Peru.

Ice-free corridors open up across the Bering Strait *c.*40,000 to *c.*20,000 years ago, but there is no evidence that humans entered the New World until the late stages of this time period.

*c.*20,000BC Migrating hunter-gatherers, using stone-, bone-, wood- and shell-tool technologies, probably entered the New World from north-east Asia.

from *c.*15,000 years ago Palaeoindians migrated south and east to populate North and South America, reaching Monte Verde in southern Chile *c.*14,850 years ago.

*c.*8500–5000BC Andean and Altiplano hunter-gatherers occupy cave and rock shelter sites in the Andes (e.g. Pachamachay, Guitarrero, Tres Ventanas and Toquepala caves). Evidence of tending of hemp-like fibre, medicinal plants, herbs and wild tubers.

*c.*6000BC–*c.*5500BC The first true monumental structures, two long parallel mounds, are built at Nanchoc, a late Archaic Period valley in the Zana Valley, north-west Peru.

by 5000BC plant domestication, as opposed to tending wild plants, is truly underway in the highlands.

*c.*5000BC The Chinchorros peoples make the first deliberately mummified burials in the Atacama Desert.

PRECERAMIC / FORMATIVE PERIOD (3500–1800BC)

Above: Alpaca grazing in the Valle de Coloa. Camelids were herded c.3500–1800BC.

This period is sometimes also called the Cotton Preceramic.

*c.*3500–1800BC True plant domestication of cotton, squashes, gourds, beans, maize, potatoes, sweet potatoes and chillies. Llamas and other camelids herded on the Altiplano.

*c.*3500BC Valdivians found Real Alto.

*c.*3200BC First ceramics made by Valdivian farmers in coastal Ecuador.

by 3000BC the full range of major food plants is grown in the highlands and the guinea pig is bred for meat.

*c.*3000BC Coastal villages such as Huaca Prieta flourish, producing early textiles.

*c.*2700BC Early northern coastal civic-ceremonial centres at Aspero – Huaca de los Idolos and Huaca de los Sacrificios.

by 2500BC the llama and alpaca have been truly domesticated.

*c.*2500BC Clay figurines at Huaca de los Idolos, Aspero.

*c.*2500–2000BC Large raised mound platforms constructed at El Paraíso, La Galagada and Kotosh.

*c.*2000BC Carved gourds at Huaca Prieta. Earliest coastal and highland pottery. Loom and heddle weaving begins.

INITIAL PERIOD (1800–750BC)

Above: The U-shaped ceremonial centre of Chavín de Huántar began c.900BC.

Spread of pottery, irrigation agriculture, monumental architecture, religious processions and ritual decapitation.

from *c.*1800BC Sophisticated irrigation systems developed in coastal oases, valleys, the highlands and Altiplano.

*c.*1800BC Construction at Moxeke includes colossal adobe heads.

*c.*1750BC Builders at La Florida bring the first pottery to this region.

*c.*1500BC Cerro Sechín flourishes as a major highland town.

*c.*1500BC Earliest Andean gold foil made at Waywaka, Peruvian highlands.

*c.*1459–1150BC Hammered gold and copper foil at Mina Perdida, coastal Peru.

*c.*1400–1200BC Sechín Alto becomes the largest U-shaped civic-ceremonial centre in the New World.

*c.*1300BC The five platform mounds at Cardál are erected.

*c.*1200BC Carved lines of warriors at Cerro Sechín show regional conflict.

*c.*1000BC The El Paraíso Tradition flourishes in the Rimac Valley.

*c.*900BC Earliest U-shaped ceremonial complex at Chavín de Huántar begins.

EARLY HORIZON (750–200BC)

Above: The Paracas Peninsula, which was a necropolis site for several settlements.

Religious cults develop around Chavín de Huántar and Pukará. Decapitation, hallucinogenic drug use and ancestor worship become widespread.

*c.*800BC Sechín Alto abandoned as a ceremonial centre.

from *c.*750BC The Old Temple at Chavín established as a cult centre. Influence of the Lanzón deity and the Staff Deity spreads. The Paracas Peninsula serves as a necropolis site, and the Oculate Being is depicted on textiles and ceramics.

*c.*500BC Construction of the New Temple at Chavín de Huántar begins.

*c.*500BC Earliest known fired-clay discs for pottery vessel making, Paracas.

*c.*400–200BC The Old Temple at Chavín enlarged to create the New Temple. The Chavín Cult spreads, especially at Kuntur Wasi and Karwa (Paracas).

*c.*400BC Annual rainfall levels fall in the Titicaca Basin. Pukará becomes centre of the Yaya-Mama Cult.

*c.*350 to 200BC Highland regional conflict evident in fortress-building in the Santa, Casma and Nepeña valleys.

*c.*250BC Beginning of the first settlement at Tiwanaku in the Titicaca Basin.

*c.*200BC Influence of Chavín Cult wanes.

EARLY INTERMEDIATE PERIOD (200BC–AD600)

Above: Construction of the Moche Huaca del Sol began c.AD100.

Cohesion of the Chavín Cult disintegrates, and several regional chiefdoms develop in the coastal and mountain valleys.

*c.*100BC Rise of the Nazca in the southern Peruvian coastal valleys and Cahuachi founded.

*c.*AD100 Burial of the Old Lord of Sipán in Lambayeque Valley.

*c.*AD100 Sacred ceremonial centre of Cahuachi dominates the Nazca area.

*c.*1st century AD Moche dynasty founded in the northern coastal valleys.

*c.*AD100 Construction of first temple platforms at Huaca del Sol and Huaca de la Luna at Moche begins.

*c.*AD250 Construction of first temple at Pachacamac and start of the Pachacamac Cult. Major construction of temple platforms at Tiwanaku begins.

*c.*AD300 Burial of the Lord of Sipán in Lambayeque Valley.

AD300–550 Several Moche regional cities founded at Huancaco, Pamapa de los Incas, Pañamarca and Mocollope.

*c.*AD500 The Moche ceremonial platforms of the Huacas del Sol and de la Luna were the largest in the area.

*c.*AD700 Moche/Nazca power wanes.

MIDDLE HORIZON (AD600–1000)

Above: View of wall and monolithic stelae, Semi-Subterranean Court, Tiwanaku.

Much of the Andean Area unified in two empires: Tiwanaku in the south and Wari in the north.

*c.*AD200 Major phase of monumental construction begins at Tiwanaku.

*c.*AD250 Settlement at Huari founded.

*c.*AD300 Major construction of central ceremonial plaza at Tiwanaku begins.

*c.*AD400–750 Elite residential quarters at Tiwanaku built. Tiwanaku colonies established at San Pedro Atacama, Omo and in the Cochabamba Valley.

*c.*AD500 Major construction at Huari and beginning of domination of the central highlands by the Wari Empire.

*c.*AD550 Pampa Grande flourishes, ruled by Sicán Lords.

by *c.*AD600 the cities of Huari and Tiwanaku dominate the highlands, building empires in the central and highlands Altiplano, respectively.

*c.*AD650 Wari city of Pikillacta founded, and Wari colonies established at Jincamocco, Azángaro, Viracochapampa and Marca Huamachuco.

*c.*AD750–1000 Third major phase of palace building begins at Tiwanaku.

*c.*AD850–900 Pikillacta abandoned.

LATE INTERMEDIATE PERIOD (AD1000–1400)

Above: View of present-day Cuzco and the Cuzco Valley where the Incas settled.

An era of political break-up is characterized by the rise of new city-states, including Lambayeque, Chimú and Pachacamac, the Colla and Lupaka kingdoms, and numerous city-states in the central and southern Andean valleys.

*c.*AD900–950 Rise of the Lambayeque-Sicán state in northern coastal Peru. Burial of the Sicán Lords at Lambayeque. Sicán capital city at Batán Grande.

*c.*AD950 Sediments of Lake Titicaca show evidence of decreased rainfall and start of a long period of drought leading to the eventual demise of Tiwanaku.

*c.*AD900 Chan Chan, capital of the Chimú, founded in the Moche Valley.

*c.*AD1000 Tiwanaku and Wari empires wane as regional political rivalry reasserts itself.

*c.*AD1000 Huari city-state abandoned.

*c.*1100 The Incas under Manco Capac, migrate into the Cuzco Valley, found Cuzco and establish the Inca dynasty.

*c.*1250 City of Tiwanaku abandoned, perhaps because of changes in climate.

*c.*1300 Sinchi Roca becomes the first emperor to use the title Sapa Inca.

*c.*1350 The Chimú conquer the Lambayeque-Sicán peoples.

LATE HORIZON (AD1400–1532)

Above: Inca stonework is distinctive in style and among the finest in the world.

In little more than 130 years the Incas build a huge empire, from Colombia to mid-Chile and from the rainforest to the Pacific and establish an imperial cult centred on Inti, the sun god, whose representative on Earth was the Sapa Inca.

*c.*1425 Viracocha, the eighth ruler, begins the Inca conquests and domination of the Cuzco Valley.

1438 Pachacuti Inca Yupanqui defeats the Chancas to dominate the Cuzco Valley and begin the expansion of the Inca Empire both within and outside the valley.

1438–71 Pachacuti begins his rebuilding of Cuzco as the imperial capital to the plan of a crouching puma, with the fortress and sun temple of Sacsahuaman forming the puma's head.

*c.*1450 Pachacuti establishes the city of Machu Picchu.

c.1462 Pachacuti begins the conquest of the Kingdom of Chimú.

1471 The Incas conquer the Kingdom of Chimú.

1471–93 Inca Tupac Yupanqui expands the empire west and south, doubling its size – north as far as the present-day Ecuador–Colombia border and south into the Titicaca Basin.

Above: The city of Machu Picchu, founded by Pachacuti c.1450.

1493–1526 Huayna Capac consolidates the empire, building fortresses, road systems, storage redistribution and religious precincts throughout the provinces. The provincial city of Qenqo is founded.

1526 Huayna Capac dies of smallpox without an agreed successor.

1526–32 Huayna Capac's son Huáscar seizes the throne but is challenged by his brother Atahualpa. A six-year civil war ends in the capture of Huáscar.

1530 Inca Empire at its greatest extent, and the largest territory in the world.

1532 Francisco Pizarro lands with a small Spanish army on the north coast of the Inca Empire and marches to meet Atahualpa at Cajamarca. He exploits the disruption of the civil war to play one claimant against the other.

1532 The Spaniards defeat the Incas at the Battle of Cajamarca and capture Atahualpa, holding him for ransom.

1533 Atahualpa condemned in a rigged Spanish trial and executed for adultery and idolatry.

1535 Francisco Pizarro founds Lima as his capital in Spanish Peru.

1541 Pizarro assassinated in his palace at Lima by Almagro and his associates.

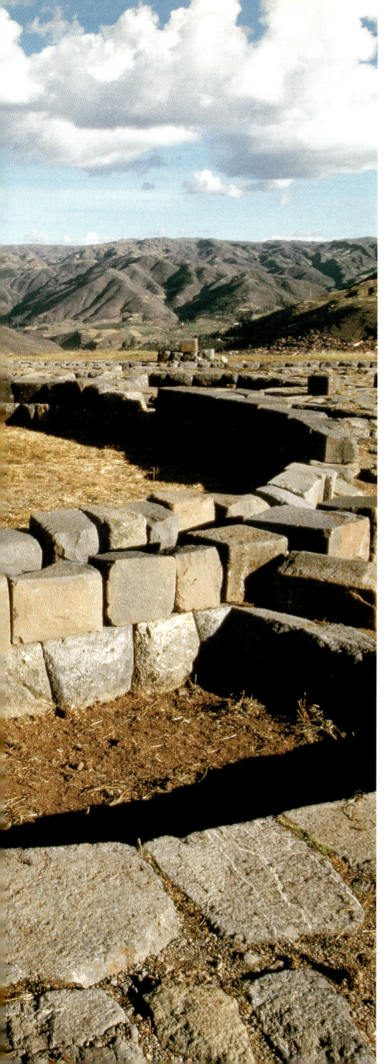

CHAPTER ONE

ARCHITECTURE

Ancient Andean builders tended to use materials as close to hand as possible. Thus, coastal peoples regularly built with mud – or adobe – bricks, while highland peoples favoured stone. Cobbles and rough field stones were also used, often plastered with mud or clay. Little is known of quarrying techniques until Inca sources, but quarrying consisted mostly of collecting from convenient sources rather than actually cutting the stone from outcrops.

Monumental architecture emphasized power and authority. The use of materials that had to be imported also enhanced prestige and indicated superior social standing. So, too, did elaborate decoration on buildings and walls. Monumental architecture, both in size and complexity of form, appeared at around 2700BC in the Andean Area and developed early traditions that lasted through to Inca times. Each successive culture copied and borrowed from predecessors, but also developed its own distinctive innovations.

From the beginning, much Andean architecture was devoted to religious purposes and themes. It was used to worship the gods, reflect the sacred landscape and impress human populations. There were cults, annual religious rituals, pilgrimage and oracle sites. Open and restricted spaces controlled participation in ritual, creating uniformity and mystery, through form and layout.

The architecture involved a variety of decorative techniques and styles: plastering, stone facing, stone carving, plaster carving, mud moulding and mural painting, as well as the combination of several techniques together.

Left: The stone architecture of the circular Temple to Inti, sun god of the Incas, forms the head in Cuzco's crouching puma.

STONE QUARRYING AND WORKING

One of the most recognizable Inca skills was their mastery of stoneworking. Their use of large, dressed stone blocks follows a 4,000-year history of the use of stone architecture, beginning with the first stone-clad platform mounds of the Preceramic Period.

QUARRIES

The Inca, and presumably pre-Inca, builders did not quarry building stone in the modern sense: they did not cut blocks from rock faces or detach sections of bedrock by undercutting. Instead, quarries were established at scree faces or prised loose from fragmented rock faces.

Blocks weighing 5 tons (tonnes) or more were roughly dressed at quarries by being hammered with river cobbles (hammerstones) before being transported to construction sites. Smaller blocks were dressed on five of their six faces, then transported for refined dressing and fitting at building sites. Quarry sites are littered with whole and shattered hammerstones, which were brought from riverbeds and were selected for their shape and hardness.

Most stone for building construction was obtained locally, or from as near as possible. By contrast, stone for sculpture was imported from greater distances when special stone was wanted, because it was precious, or because it was a desired colour or texture, or exotic or valuable in some other way. For example, as early as the Preceramic Period, coastal peoples imported small amounts of obsidian (a natural volcanic glass) from highland sources hundreds of kilometres (miles) away for superior or more prestigious knives and other tools. The Late Horizon Inca central plaza of Haucaypata–Cusipata in Cuzco was covered with a layer of sand imported from the coast.

Several Inca quarries are known, for example at Kachiqhata near Ollantaytambo, for that site and perhaps earlier constructions, and at outcrops just north of Sacsahuaman.

TRANSPORT

Ancient Andean transport was on human and animal backs. There were no transport vehicles, as the wheel was unknown and llamas are notoriously adverse to pulling. Transporting goods through mountains in vehicles would also have required an extensive road system – not just trunk roads connecting major cities, but more than just pathways within and between local communities.

Above: Inca stonemasons fitting blocks on a wall, depicted in Poma de Ayala's Nueva Corónica, *c.1615.*

These methods were unsuitable for transporting stone blocks. Instead, gangs of men dragged the blocks with ropes, on the ground or possibly on log rollers or sledges. Earth and cobble ramps were built at quarries to drag stone blocks down; other ramps at construction sites enabled blocks to be hauled into position. Ramps at Sacsahuaman were levelled after construction, but some ramps were left at Sillustani near Lake Titicaca.

STONEWORKING

Inca stonework is remarkable for its huge stone building blocks, which were carefully and painstakingly fitted together by matching angle for angle at the points of contact between blocks, so that no mortar was needed to hold them together. The oft-repeated phrase that not even a knife blade can be slid between blocks

Left: Closely fitted block stonework at Tambo Machay hunting lodge. Multiple trapezoidal niches and steep staircased passages form solid blocks that 'sympathize' with the landscape.

describes their precision. Withstanding 500 years of earthquakes also shows the strength of their construction. Earthquakes often destroy most modern houses, leaving only Inca buildings and foundations standing.

Precise fitting was used only on the most important buildings: temples, administrative offices and palaces. For other buildings techniques were less recognizably Inca, but continued methods developed for millennia and used local, undressed stone or adobe blocks (mud bricks).

Such strength is also true of Inca terracing and irrigation systems. Despite being in an active volcanic region, Inca terraced fields and irrigation conduits continue to be used.

As with almost everything else in Andean civilization, construction was related to and intimate with the landscape.

SHAPING TECHNIQUES

The careful fitting of Inca fine masonry walls was achieved by laboriously pecking the surfaces with harder stone 'hammers' and chiselling with bronze tools. The rock surface was more shattered and ground away than cut, but

unwanted stone could also be sheared away by hitting the face with glancing blows. Grinding with smooth stones and perhaps wet sand (although there is no evidence of smooth polishing) achieved final fitting. Inca blocks retain the small pitting left by these methods.

Blocks were usually of various shapes, but for the most important buildings uniform rectangular prism or cube blocks were fitted in courses like bricks. Varyingly shaped blocks were dressed along their edges to fit snugly, and used especially when very large blocks were fitted, such as on massive walls for terracing or stabilizing riverbanks. The final grinding and fitting of stone blocks on refined buildings were done *in situ*, and therefore blocks must have had to be lifted and taken down repeatedly to

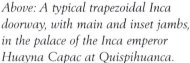

Above: A typical trapezoidal Inca doorway, with main and inset jambs, in the palace of the Inca emperor Huayna Capac at Quispihuanca.

achieve their exact fit. Corners were made strong by interlocking header and stretcher construction.

Inca engineers used plumb-bobs and two-stick slide rules for positioning and possibly for transcribing the shape of one face to another as a template. Bronze and wooden levers and crowbars were used to manoeuvre blocks.

LABOUR

These tedious and time-consuming methods suggest the massive labour forces needed to complete masonry work. Specialist engineers and skilled stonemasons did the fine work, but the tasks of quarrying or collecting, hauling and rough shaping involved large gangs, as did the making of earthen ramps for raising stones up to higher courses. Construction was one of the tasks that could be assigned to workers in the *mit'a* tax draft. The chronicler Pedro de Ondegardo recorded that as many as 20 men could work for an entire year on dressing and fitting some of the largest stone blocks.

Left: The most famous Inca stone – the 12-cornered, carefully fitted block in a monolithic wall on Hatun Rumiyoc Street, Cuzco. The base is a single side, the right and left sides have three angles each, and the top no fewer than five.

MONUMENTAL ARCHITECTURE

The size and monumental nature of ancient Andean architecture is undoubtedly impressive, and this is true even when most of the features are flattened and only the foundations survive.

FIRST MONUMENTAL STRUCTURES

Large-scale monumental architecture began as early as 2700BC, in the Preceramic Period. In the Initial Period, from *c*.2000BC, at a time when the use of ceramics and other technological innovations (including irrigation canals) was beginning, ceremonial centres were built throughout coastal and highland river valleys. It was the beginning of large-scale public architecture, including huge individual monuments, and extensive and complex ceremonial compounds. These were some of the largest structures ever built in the Americas.

These centres were monuments to the gods and their purpose was for religious gatherings. They were not cities, for there were few associated dwellings and they lacked the density of buildings and area coverage characteristic of cities, but as focuses of public labour and worship they provided the core idea that later became

Below: Machu Picchu. Inca architecture followed a long tradition of 'fitting' the landscape. In mountainous terrain, ridges were levelled for enclosures and buildings, while steep slopes were terraced with stone bulwarks.

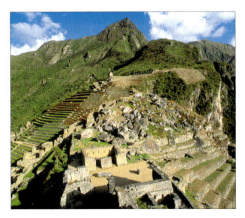

a feature of Andean cities. The few dwellings were those of resident attendants of the cults. Each ceremonial centre served groups of scattered towns and villages.

ASPERO

The earliest such ceremonial centre was Aspero (*c*.2700BC), on the northern Peruvian coast. Covering more than 12ha (30 acres) along the north bluff of the Supe River, Aspero comprised six or seven large platform mounds (4m/13ft or more high), eleven smaller mounds (1–2m/3¼–6½ft high), plus interspersed plazas and terraces. The outer walls of the mounds were faced with locally quarried stone set in mud mortar. The bulks of the mounds were built up using loose mesh bags of sedge fibre filled with rubble, cobbles and quarried stone.

EL PARAÍSO

Construction at El Paraíso, near the central Peruvian coast on the south bank and plain of the Chillón River, began *c*.2000BC. El Paraíso initiated two significant trends: settlements were established inland, a short distance from the coast, and their general plans took the shape of a U. El Paraíso covered 50ha (125 acres) or more and its builders used about

Above: Huaca de la Luna, Moche. Whatever the building materials – adobe bricks or colossal stone blocks – Andean architects aspired to imposing, monumental structures for their ceremonial centres.

100,000 tons (tonnes) of quarried stone to make platform mounds and other buildings. The two largest mounds are each about 50m (165ft) wide and run parallel for 400m (¼ mile) to form the sides of the U-plan, enclosing a 7ha (17 acre) plaza. The base of the U was formed by a building of 50sq m (540sq ft), 8m (25ft) high, with two stairways.

KOTOSH AND LA GALGADA

In the highlands, at about the same time, monumental architecture was not so grand in scale, but provided the same function of public focus. At Kotosh, the Temple of the Crossed Hands was a square chamber on a raised platform, one of two mounds at the site. At La Galgada there were also two temple mounds, flanking a circular court.

THE BIG ONES

The heyday of U-shaped ceremonial structures began *c*.1500BC, and it is estimated that these centres had about 1,000

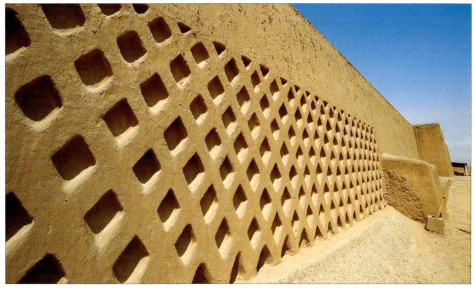

residents each. Up to the beginning of the Early Horizon and the ascendancy of Chavín de Huántar, three monumental architectural traditions developed at coastal sites, representing culturally related regions of independent ceremonial centres and their communities. These were the U-shaped ceremonial centres of the south-central Peruvian coast, the rectangular mound and circular forecourt complexes of the north-central coast, and the low-platform complexes of the northern coast.

Sites include La Florída, Cardál, Sechín Alto, Pampa de las Llamas–Moxeke, Las Haldas, Cerro Sechín, Caballo Muerto, Cupisnique and many others. Sechín Alto and Moxeke were the largest U-shaped complexes ever built in the Andean Area: nearly 1.5km (just under 1 mile) and 1km (just over ½ mile) long, respectively. By comparison, the Las Haldas U-shaped complex was c.440m (less than ½ mile) long.

MONUMENTALITY WITHIN CITIES
The monumental tradition started in the late Preceramic and Initial periods continued through the remainder of Andean prehistory. Early Horizon people continued to build ceremonial centres of platforms and plazas, exemplified by Chavín de Huántar and the Nazca centre of Cahuachi.

From about the middle of the Early Horizon (c.500BC), the complexity of sites began to include the variation in structures, craft specialization, social hierarchy and population densities characteristic of cities. Early Intermediate Period architecture included the huge platforms of the Moche, which were seemingly attempts to build miniature mountains on the coast in honour of the gods of the distant inland peaks.

Monumental architecture in the Middle Horizon, exemplified by Tiwanaku and Huari, show this continuity in large, high platforms in combination with rectangular ceremonial plazas. Tiwanaku featured huge monolithic gateways, and introduced the innovations of standard units of measurements, blocks prepared ready to fit, and grooves for using ropes to manoeuvre them into

Above: Wall of the Tschudi ciudadela, Chan Chan of the Chimú. Fine river-laid silts in the western coastal valleys provided abundant material for poured-mud walls to create huge compounds, elaborately moulded and carved.

position and hold them with T- or I-shaped metal clamps. Wari architecture developed a military-like precision of grid planning, built with huge cut-stone blocks.

Late Intermediate Period cities, such as Pachacamac, Chan Chan, Batán Grande and La Centinela, to name but a few, were huge complexes of compounds, plazas and administrative buildings surrounded by dense populations in suburban housing.

Late Horizon Inca monumental architecture is self-evident. From the city of Cuzco and its temple-fortress of Sacsahuaman through the mountain retreat of Machu Picchu to the numerous Inca provincial capitals, monumental and ceremonial architecture was built to impose and advertise Inca power. Huge blocks of stone were shaped to fit together without mortar and to build massive walls for temples and other public buildings, and for agricultural terracing and the encasement of rivers in Cuzco.

Left: Sacsahuaman, Cuzco. Inca architects frequently used the base rock itself to shape monumental structures, almost seamlessly integrating such stonework into the parts constructed from colossal cut and shaped stones.

RITUAL FOCUS

The organized nature of Inca cities and their focus on religious ritual did not develop suddenly, but began with the first Preceramic monumental architecture. Organization of space as a perception of the universe and as a reflection of the landscape was endemic in Andean architectural form.

The development of U-shaped ceremonial centres, pyramidal platforms, sunken courtyards and clustered temple chambers around courts were fundamental Andean architectural forms. People in different regions developed different forms, singly or in combinations. Such forms reflected the essence of religious belief and how religious ritual was conducted, and the shape of the landscape in which the beliefs developed. The forms endured throughout Andean ancient history.

THE U-SHAPED PLAN

During the Initial Period, the U-shaped plan developed in in the northern coastal cultures, spread into the adjacent mountainous regions, and might be regarded as reaching its fullest expression at Chavín de Huántar, where the holy city seems to have been located deliberately between

Below: Worshippers' attention in Moche's ritual enclosures was directed to lurid murals. Here the Decapitator God stares menacingly from a wall of the Huaca de la Luna, Moche.

coast and high sierra. Combined with sunken courtyards and labyrinthine interiors, the temple fulfilled a third religious function: that of a pilgrimage centre.

The U-shaped form endured into the Late Horizon. It was used in miniature at Chan Chan, within the *ciudadela* compounds of the Chimú rulers.

CONTROL

The focus on ritual in ceremonial centres and urban ceremonial precincts included public and private architectural elements. The key was an emphasis on control.

Religious ritual became highly structured. The nature and layout of structures at ceremonial centres and city precincts suggest that they guided public processions along designated routes. Inca Cuzco had a radiating set of sacred pathways, called *ceque* lines, for religious observation. They were the routes followed by priests in leading religious processions, by initiates in coming-of-age rituals, and by sacrificial victims on their way out of the city.

Similarly, of more ancient date, the Nazca lines in the deserts of southern coastal Peru were pathways for religious procession. It has been suggested that they were even sometimes purpose-built

Above: The Nazca lines of Peru's southern coastal deserts reveal the early development of ancient Andean ritual focus in architecture.

for a single event, and that the pathways along individual figures and geometric shapes belonged to specific kinship groups.

VARIOUS STRUCTURES

Elements of ceremonial complexes reveal different aspects of religious ceremony. There were specific areas for large gatherings, in which the general public was clearly meant to congregate and in which their level of participation was accommodated. Other areas were equally clearly built to restrict participation in religious worship to a privileged few.

PLAZAS

Huge areas, plazas and courts, enclosed by large platforms or walls, characterized Initial Period U-shaped ceremonial centres and platform mound complexes in the Early Horizon and Early Intermediate Period. Chavín de Huántar's two succeeding temples each wrapped themselves around an open-ended courtyard for crowds. The ceremonial cores of Moche cities and the pilgrimage city of Pachacamac on the central Peruvian coast were formed of intricate collections of large and small courtyards for large and small gatherings.

The Middle Horizon Moche successors at Pampa Grande surrounded the dominant platform mound of Huaca Fortaleza with a complex of large walled courts and more open plazas beyond them. The singular walled enclosure at Galindo comprised a large court with a sunken rectangular court within it. In Wari cities large public plazas were enclosed within grid-planned walls and streets. At Tiwanaku the Akapana temple platform fronted a large, open plaza.

Late Intermediate Period cities continued the tradition. Sicán Batán Grande's ceremonial precinct comprised large open plazas defined by clusters of platform mounds and other buildings, reminiscent of Pampa Grande. Each *ciudadela* compound at the Chimú capital Chan Chan included a large courtyard within high walls, separated from the highly subdivided area beyond. There were similar courts at Tucume Viejo, where the compounds were anchored around the Huaca Larga platform and the huge, artificially stepped peak

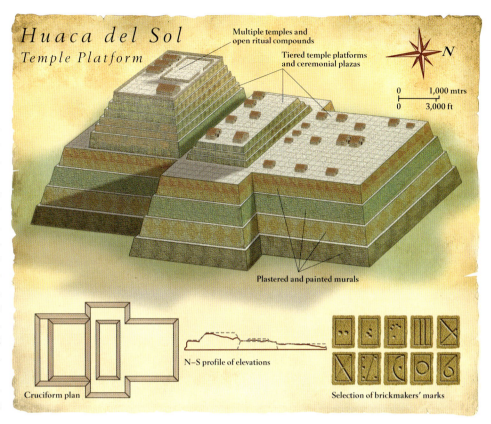

Huaca del Sol
Temple Platform

Multiple temples and open ritual compounds

Tiered temple platforms and ceremonial plazas

0   1,000 mtrs
0   3,000 ft

Plastered and painted murals

Cruciform plan

N–S profile of elevations

Selection of brickmakers' marks

Below: The Kalasasaya and Semi-Subterranean Court at Tiwanaku, where rulers and priests performed their rituals.

of La Raya. The ceremonial precinct at Chincha La Centinela comprised walled courts and low platforms clustered around a dominant higher platform mound.

Inca cities included large plazas with *ushnu* platforms for observing and addressing gathered crowds.

RESTRICTIONS
The counterparts to public areas were smaller courts, sunken courts and enclosed rooms. These were an equally long-lived tradition. They began in the subdivided buildings atop platforms at

Above: Reconstruction of Huaca del Sol temple, Moche, showing ground plan, north–south elevations and brickmakers' marks.

sites such as Kotosh, La Galgada, Huaca de los Reyes, Cerro Sechín and many others in northern and central Peru. Farther south, Chiripa in the Titicaca Basin exemplifies a tradition of single-roomed buildings surrounding a courtyard atop a low platform.

In later periods the intricately subdivided temples of Chavín de Huántar and Pachacamac, through to the complexes of rooms at Chan Chan and the Coricancha temple of Inca Cuzco, were meant to restrict the performance and observance of religious ritual to a select few.

Between these two extremes, combinations of plazas containing sunken courtyards, fronted by platform mounds supporting temples, reveal the controlled nature of ancient Andean religious ceremony. Participants were gathered, then led in managed processions along prescribed routes into and through sunken courts or other restricted areas, before priests and selected individuals mounted the platforms to perform special rites within private temples.

LABYRINTHINE SECRETS

Restriction of intimate religious ritual to selected individuals formed the counterpart to great public extravaganzas. The Incas impressed their subjects with glittering spectacles and public addresses to advertise and emphasize their power. As in other spheres, they were following Wari and Tiwanaku practice in a long-lived tradition of public ceremony.

PUBLIC AND PRIVATE RITUAL

From the Initial Period onwards the importance of religion as a driving force in the development of cities nurtured the growing power of the priesthood. Religious influence in everyday life was exemplified in the development and spread of cults, three of the most famous being those of Chavín, Pachacamac and Inca Inti.

Priestly power and control were revealed in the secretive nature of some elements of worship and the restriction of some rituals to selected individuals or as private events.

PRIVATE ROOMS

Constructions of platforms supporting subdivided temples began towards the end of the Preceramic Period and flourished in the Initial Period. The Temple of the Crossed Hands at Kotosh, the round-cornered chambers at La Galgada, the

Above: New Temple gateway, Chavín de Huántar. Not all ritual was witnessed by crowds of worshippers, as much took place within inner chambers whose passages were known only to the priests.

chambered compounds atop the Huaca de los Idolos and Huaca de los Sacrificios at Aspero, and the complex of interconnected rooms at El Paraíso all typify the development of intricate temple interiors.

The importance of religious figures, whether priest-kings or separate from the rulers, developed early and grew in strength through Andean civilization. The extent of cults was relatively localized until the Chavín Cult spread an unprecedented religious unity in the Early Horizon. Chavín de Huántar became a pilgrimage centre to which people came from great distances to consult the oracle of its chief deity.

Intimate religious practice is suggested by the labyrinthine nature of Chavín de Huántar's temples, Old and New. While the platform arms of each temple embrace a circular (Old Temple) and square (New Temple) sunken court, the

Left: The Lanzón carved stone monolith, Chavín de Huántar. Hidden deep within the multi-storeyed chambers at the back of the Old Temple, it served as an oracle chamber and place of ritual bloodletting, channelled and pooled by grooves and a dish carved in the notched stone.

Right: Entrance to the Semi-Subterranean Court, Tiwanaku. The central ceremonial core formed a complex of temple mounds and enclosed courts for more intimate rituals.

temple interiors comprise mysterious dark corridors connecting inner rooms and chambers, water conduits and niches. Its courts and plazas could hold 1,500 worshippers, while its inner chambers had room for a mere fraction as many.

ORACLES AND ROARING TEMPLES

A staircase rises from the Old Temple plaza in alignment with steps into and out of the sunken circular court. Crowds could participate in ritual and processions in the plaza and circular court, but could hardly do so inside the temple's constricted spaces. A corridor leads to an inner two-storey chamber within which stood the Lanzón Stela, the chief idol. The floor of the chamber above its base is holed to accommodate the notched upper portion of the stela, and it is suggested that a priest could conceal himself in the upper chamber to act as the voice of the deity to pronounce oracles.

The increasing status of the Chavín Cult was shown by more than doubling the temple's size with the addition of the New Temple *c.*500BC. Further secrecy was

incorporated because no staircase leads to the top of the New Temple terraces. Stairs led only to a platform and square court before the Black and White Portal on the first terrace. Instead, priests could appear mysteriously on the top terrace, or at two rectangular 'reverse balconies' above the Black and White Portal via interior stairs.

The Old and New temples were used together, maintaining the continuity of the deities and cult, and the elaborate interior chambers were multipurpose. Ritual paraphernalia and stores of manufactured and exotic goods were probably kept in niches and smaller chambers. It has also been suggested that some chambers were hermit-like cells for priests and temple attendants. It is also thought that the winding conduits and shafts served the dual purpose both of ventilation and as conduits through which to flush water and cause a roaring noise to echo through the empty corridors – a noise that could have its pitch modulated by the opening and closing of ventilation ducts.

Such measures, together with oracular status, certainly would have enhanced and perpetuated Chavín as a centre of supernatural power and authority.

Left: Temple of the Moon. For more than a millennium Pachacamac was a centre of pilgrimage and worship, focused on its oracle temple, and replete with additions of new temples, courts and accommodations for pilgrims.

PATIOS AND COMPOUNDS

The tradition of controlled worship was obvious at Tiwanaku as well. At Tiwanaku, instead of enclosed chambers, worship was regulated by a complex of open-air plazas, platforms with sunken courts and semi-subterranean courtyards. The elements were linked by monumental gateways marking the boundaries of sacred spaces and isolation atop the Akapana temple platform, thus restricting who entered and how many could participate.

At the sacred oracle site of Pachacamac (from the 1st century AD) the Pachacamac idol and oracle was housed in a small temple atop a platform mound. Its isolation and size restricted it to worship by a few people at a time. North and west of the oracle temple were ramped platforms and an elaborate complex of room suites, passages and small patios around larger courtyards. These were quarters, halls and sacred spaces in which pilgrims could worship in small groups.

Finally, in the imperial compounds of Chimú kings at Chan Chan, walled off from large courtyards, were the intricate complexes of miniature U-shaped ceremonial precincts and seeming mazes of large and small rooms, niches, store blocks and palaces of the dead rulers, each an inner city within greater Chan Chan.

ARCHITECTURAL DECORATION

Ancient Andean stone and mud-brick constructions were often highly embellished. Decorations included stone facing, mud plaster, adobe-brick friezes, sculpting in poured mud and mural-painting on walls.

Traces of paint on walls have been found at some of the earliest coastal and highland sites. Common Inca practice was to plaster cobble- and fieldstone walls with mud and then paint them. Tambo Colorado, a typical example, has traces of red and yellow ochre paint surviving on its adobe walls.

According to Spanish chroniclers, the Incas covered the interior walls of the Coricancha temple with sheets of gold!

PAINTED WALLS

The earliest evidence of wall painting and sculpting was discovered at Aspero, on the central Peruvian coast. The platform mound of Huaca de los Idolos supported a series of room complexes, one replacing the other through continuous use. The rough stone walls were mud-plastered and some were painted red or yellow. Passageways lead from a main court to more private chambers behind it, one of which is decorated with a white clay frieze of five parallel horizontal bands, clapboard-like. There are also plastered benches and cubical niches around some walls.

Below: Huaca de la Luna, Moche. Worshippers were constantly reminded of the gods in vivid murals of the Decapitator God.

Above: Huaca de la Luna, Moche. Colourful murals on the courtyard walls included rows of figures holding hands.

Paint was also found on the walls of the Temple of the Crossed Hands at highland Kotosh. A stylized white serpent was painted on the stairway leading to the temple, and the entryway was painted red. Inside, two sets of crossed hands were sculpted into the yellow-brown mud-plaster below cubical niches. It is thought that they represent a male and female pair, characteristically exemplifying Andean duality.

EARLY MURALS

The Initial Period U-shaped ceremonial complex of Garagay, on the central Peruvian coast, has one of the most remarkable early wall friezes in its Middle Temple. Running the length and height of the walls, low-relief mud-brick sculpturing shows a fanged face with a whorl (an arachnid pedipalp or mucus secretion?) within spider web-like cross-hatching; a long-bodied insect with a human head; and two facing fanged faces. Stylized geometric motifs separate each figure, and traces of bright red, blue, yellow and white paint were found on the various elements. The insect probably represents shamanistic transformation.

Early murals were also found on the walls of the earliest (*c.*1800BC) building phases at Cerro Sechín. Exterior walls were painted pink, interior walls blue, and the entryway to the main chamber had a mural of large black felines with red-orange

paws and white claws on a yellow background. The main façade of the second-phase temple had clay friezes and multicoloured incised line figures, including an upside-down human with closed eyes and blood streaming from the head.

MOCHE MURALS

Early Intermediate Period Moche sites are famous for their murals. A mural on Huaca de la Luna's Platform III walls

Below: The massive poured-mud walls at Chan Chan of the Chimú were elaborately moulded and carved with repetitious motifs.

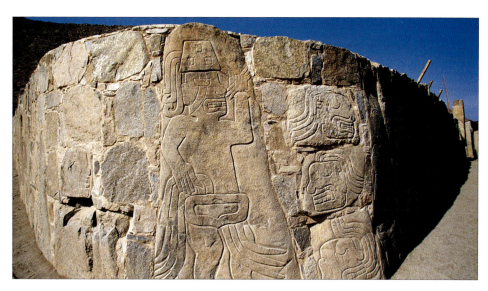

Right: Cerro Sechín commemorated a military victory or a ritual battle in low-relief on slabs forming a wall around the temple complex.

shows the story of the 'Revolt of the Objects', in which inanimate objects counter depictions of ordinary humans: a warrior with a fox's head, a boat with legs, a ceremonial staff with legs and arms chasing a fallen warrior. It appears to be a mythological portrayal of chaos, a story that was told to Spanish chroniclers at the time of the conquest.

Walls in the Great Patio of Platform I feature a grimacing, fanged face with bulging red-and-black-rimmed eyes and curling black hair and beard. The face is of a sea god or the Decapitator, set within a diamond frame and surrounded by stepped-motif figures with red-and-white-circle eyes. Another wall depicts a line of Moche warriors.

Now-destroyed murals at Pañamarca (Mural E), south of Moche, showed part of 'The Sacrifice Ceremony', led by a priestess holding a goblet and followed by a procession of smaller figures presenting goblets, plus a crawling, fanged and forked-tongued serpent. It represents the conclusion of Moche ritual combat by sacrifice of the loser and 'The Presentation Ceremony'.

PACHACAMAC AND CHANCAY

Mud-plastered walls at coastal sites were the ideal medium for mural-painting. The Middle Horizon and Late Intermediate Period temple mound terrace walls of Pachacamac were once covered in bright murals, repainted up to 16 times. Plants and animals were depicted in bright reds, blues, greens, yellows and whites, emphasizing the natural abundance of the long-lived pilgrimage city in its fertile river valley. Reed and human-hair brushes were found near one of the terraces.

At Cerro Trinidad, one long adobe wall was painted in four colours with interlaced fish – a design used on Chancay pottery.

STONE WARRIORS

The carving of stone friezes along walls was another characteristic form of Andean architectural decoration. One of the earliest and most famous is the great wall surrounding the temple complex at Initial Period Cerro Sechín. A wall of more than 300 upright slabs comprises alternating tall single slabs and shorter stacks of small slabs. Each is carved in low relief with incised lines. The tall slabs show triumphant warriors wearing pillbox hats and brandishing war clubs or staffs of authority. Stacks of smaller slabs between them display their mutilated victims. Some lack legs, or are twisted in painful contortions; others are mere decapitated heads with streaming hair; one shows his intestines spilling out. The figures appear to be in procession, marching around the temple to converge at the front staircase, where two tall flanking slabs depict banners. Flanking the rear stairway are two warriors holding a club and staff.

Below: Artist's reconstruction of Huaca de la Luna, Moche, and plan of the ceremonial precinct showing the relationship between the Huaca del Sol and de la Luna.

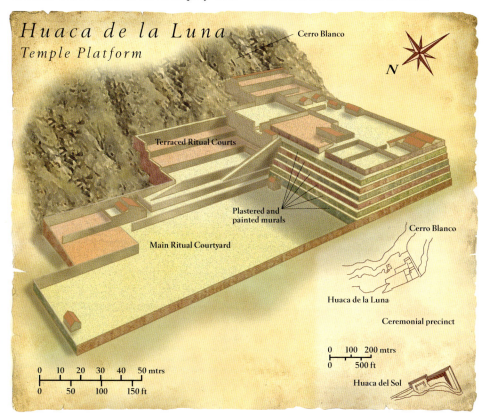

Huaca de la Luna
Temple Platform

Cerro Blanco

N

Terraced Ritual Courts

Plastered and painted murals

Main Ritual Courtyard

Cerro Blanco

Huaca de la Luna

Ceremonial precinct

0   10   20   30   40   50 mtrs
0   50   100   150 ft

0   100   200 mtrs
0   500 ft

Huaca del Sol

Not far away, and of similar date, at Moxeke a single, rectangular stone slab was found, carved on two adjacent sides. One side has a naturalistic human hand carved inside a hand-shaped depression, and the other face has a central, forked-tongue snake head with two bodies curling back on themselves in incised lines on either side of the head.

CHAVÍN TRANSFORMATIONS

The highland, Initial Period cult site of Chavín de Huántar features rows of carved stone friezes at its Old and New Temples. Portraying religious themes of shamanistic transformation, a procession of figures marches around the walls of the Old Temple's circular sunken court. An upper register of slabs has a low-relief procession of side-facing humanoid figures with fanged mouths and streaming, snake-headed hair. They wear serpentine belts, tunics and trousers. Their finger- and toenails curl in harpy eagle-like claws. One carries a San Pedro cactus branch and another a conch-shell trumpet. The register below them, separated by two rows of plain slabs, is a row of prowling jaguars on rectangular slabs.

The seven or more paired humanoid and jaguar sets depict a scene of shamans displaying the hallucinogenic cactus used for mystic ritual, and to induce transformation from human to jaguar.

Similar themes and imagery were continued in the New Temple, which more than doubled the size of the complex.

Above: Murals at Garagay depict a human-feline-serpentine face within a cross-hatched spider's web on the Middle Temple wall.

The façade forming the lowest tier of the New Temple's main platform was decorated with fully sculpted heads, mounted on the wall with tenons. Although only one was found in place, more than 40 were found during excavations.

The heads display a succession of 'states' in human transformation into beast. The mouths show successive alteration of the lips and teeth from human to feline fangs and curling sides; snouts become projected; noses become progressively flatter, with frontal nostrils; almond-shaped human eyes change to bulging round ones, weeping mucus (a characteristic reaction to drug-taking); cheeks become scarified to represent whiskers.

The heads flanked the Black and White Portal, the columns of its entrance themselves carved in low-relief with two avian figures, heads tilted back to peer straight up, and wings outspread in typical raptor hunting flight. The pair represents Andean religious duality in two ways: the north column, supporting the white (female) granite half-lintel, depicts an eagle – identifiable by an eagle's pronounced cere (nostril hole in the beak), and as female by the 'vagina dentata' between its legs; the south column, supporting the black (male) limestone half-lintel, is a hawk – identifiable as a

hawk by the band running through the eye and as male by his central frontal fang 'penis metaphor'.

TIWANAKU STONE FRIEZES

Highland Tiwanaku, whose citizens built their stone temples, platform mounds and sunken courts through the late Early Intermediate Period and Middle Horizon, also features sculptured stone decorations. Around the walls of the Semi-Subterranean Court were mounted scores of severed heads, tenoned into the walls at various heights.

Tiwanaku's builders also carved the monumental Gateway of the Sun. Made from a single huge slab measuring 3.8m (12½ft) wide and 2.8m (9ft) high, with a 1.4m (4½ft) opening, above its rebate jambs is a frieze in low- and high-relief depicting the Staff Being flanked by running 'angels'. The high-relief, central, front-facing, staff-bearing figure is the ray-headed Sun God/Staff Deity, standing on a stepped platform. Running (or flying?) towards him are three flanking rows of 48 bird-like figures, with feathered heads and wings, each holding a single staff. Beneath the whole runs a strip of geometric shapes, and flanking the entryway are two rectangular niches.

Below: Faint traces of rich temple murals at Cerro Sechín – crabs flanking the entrance to a chamber – are some of the earliest Andean murals.

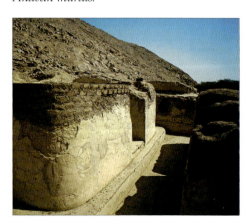

Above: Moche El Brujo includes courtyard murals with a 'dancing' figure linking hands with others.

Many other Tiwanaku monolithic wall slabs are decorated with rows of inset stepped-diamond shapes – sometimes called the 'Andean Cross' – a shape first used in the Middle Horizon and also used on textiles and by the Incas.

FORMS IN MUD AND PLASTER
The characteristic coastal use of mud-bricks and thick plastering lent itself to carving and moulding. The mud-brick painted friezes at Garagay are described above, and atop Mound A two clay sculptures of humans with circular shields were set into the terrace wall.

To announce elite power and authority, huge carved adobe sculptures adorned the faces of terraces and sunken courtyards. At Moxeke, three sculptures depicted a caped figure, a central shaman with snakes, and a grinning face. At the Huaca de los Reyes mound of Caballo Muerto, four huge adobe heads decorate the summit. Almost 2m (6ft) high, they portray human-like faces with clenched teeth, but also feline fangs, flared nostrils and gaping eyes. They were probably once painted.

Middle Horizon Moche Cao Viejo–El Brujo, in the Chicama Valley, has, on a base terrace, a frieze of 10 life-size naked prisoners, ropes around their necks, led by a warrior. The top terrace shows the legs of a spider or crab Decapitator God brandishing a *tumi* sacrificial knife. (Before its destruction by looters, its fanged mouth and double ear spools were also visible.)

POURED-MUD MOULDING
The ultimate expression in decorated mud walls are those at Chan Chan and other Chimú and Chincha cities, such as Huaca del Dragón and La Centinela.

In a riot of variations, in disciplined and regularly uniform applied forms, Chimú poured-mud walls depict all manner of creatures and geometric shapes. There are rows of identical fish, birds and other creatures, and stacked staff-bearing humanoids with animal heads. There are diamond-lattice patterns and parallel horizontal lines of moulding creating a shutter-effect. Stylized, stepped-fret fish, birds and other animals add an abstract dimension.

Huaca del Dragón features walls with rainbow-like arcs topped with curled solar flares (or waves?) framed by moulded rectangular borders. Mythical creatures support the ends of the arcs, together flanking and framing twinned, facing mythical creatures with sinuous bodies and web-like tails. Long-tailed mythical figures holding axe-bladed staffs march in a frieze above them.

Contemporary Chincha La Centinela's builders painted most of its walls brilliant white and carved them with similar high-relief friezes of birds, fish and geometric patterns.

Below: The great 'Gateway of the Sun' at Tiwanaku is perhaps the most famous single shaped and carved stone in ancient Andean civilization. It depicts a central Staff Deity flanked by numerous 'running' attendants.

INCA STRUCTURES

Inca buildings, with rare exceptions, were rectangular in plan, regardless of size, purpose or quality. Most were a single room, with one door in a long wall, or several if the building was exceptionally long. Most were single-storey, although often had a second level when built against a hillside, but in Cuzco there were two-storey and occasionally three-storey buildings. More rarely, U-shaped and round structures were built.

The standardization of form simultaneously fulfilled the goals of practicality, aesthetics, a perverse sense of 'equality' among official Inca citizens, and political power. Fineness of stonework, décor and size reinforced social hierarchy. Even the sacred Coricancha temple was a standard form – although one elevated to a higher status with sheet-gold-plated walls.

MATERIALS

Fine, fitted masonry was used only for the most important structures. Most walls were of unshaped stone set in mud mortar, using materials collected from nearby fields. Coastal buildings were of adobe blocks (mud bricks), though in the rainier highlands adobe was less practical. Both fieldstone and adobe walls were smoothed with poured mud or clay plaster, then painted.

Below: Careful interlocking precluded the need for mortar in Inca stonework; and the use of huge blocks and inclining the walls of structures made them resistant to earthquakes.

Above: Sacsahuaman. The close-fitting shaped stone blocks of the Inca Sun Temple integrate with the shape of the hill of which they form a 'natural' extension.

Roofs were of thatch, supported by wooden or cane poles, steeply sloped at an angle of about 60 degrees in highland regions to shed rain. Highland builders used *ichu* grass. Nails were unknown; the pole frames were lashed together with rope, and secured to the walls on stone pegs built into the walls. Some Inca walls also have stone rings at the gable crown.

The Incas are renowned for the fineness of their masonry dressing and for the precision of fitting. Huge blocks in the most important temples and administrative buildings were laboriously pecked, tested, removed and adjusted, then refitted until not even a knife blade could be slid into the joins. One famous block, on Hatun Rumiyoc Street, Cuzco, has 12 angled sides!

INCA FEATURES

Three notable Inca features are: battered (inclined) walls, a lack of interior room divisions (with rare exceptions) and the use of trapezoidal (narrower at top than at base) doorways, windows and wall niches.

Inca walls are inclined at an angle of 4–6 degrees from base to top, being thicker at the base. Reasons for this are uncertain. At a practical level, the incline counters the outward thrust of the roof structure, and so the walls may be more earthquake resistant. Undoubtedly, however, part of the reason was aesthetic. The visual effect, called entasis, is an appearance of greater height and refinement, making Inca walls look more imposing and so impressing and displaying power.

The significance of trapezoids is equally uncertain, but they were probably also chosen for earthquake stability and aesthetics. Many trapezoidal entrances, especially gateways to compounds, have double jambs; windows and niches are

Below: The most careful sizing, shaping and dressing was used on temples and imperial buildings, as here in the Temple of Inti at Ollantaytambo, north of Cuzco.

Right: At the country palace at Pisac, the contrast in the quality of stonework for the Intihuatana quarter (Place of the Sun) and a more ordinary building is evident.

often double-framed. Trapezoids are a central and northern feature; rectangular forms were used south of Lake Titicaca.

Dressed stone walls often have protruding stone pegs on gables and inside. Pegs are dressed stone cylinders imbedded into the masonry, or, in more important buildings, carved from single ashlar building blocks. Some are square in section. Exterior pegs were anchors for roof ties; interior pegs presumably for hanging things on them, as Inca buildings had little furniture except for wall niche repositories.

BUILDING TYPES

A *kancha* was a group of three or more rectangular buildings around an open courtyard, the whole enclosed by a wall. *Kanchas* varied in size and purpose: dwellings, temples, factories, administrative buildings, sometimes combined in the same compound. Residential *kanchas* probably housed extended families.

Kallankas were large, long buildings, often with several doorways opening into a plaza. Their size and public nature

Below: The temples of the Coricancha have some of the finest examples of dressed-stone walls and trapezoidal windows and doorways.

suggests that they were for ceremony and for housing Inca officials touring the imperial provinces.

The *ushnu* is a platform at the centre or one side of the main plaza of state settlements. It was used for state occasions as a viewing stand for rituals, reviewing troops and receiving subject leaders. Built only in Cuzco and imperial provincial cities, it was a symbol of Inca domination.

Inca public buildings – administrative *kanchas* and temples – are normally identified by their size and fine masonry, and by the use of trapezoidal doorways. These features are more readily identifiable in the Cuzco area and in the provincial capitals of the central and northern provinces, but are rare in the western and southern provinces. It seems that impressive buildings were felt important as symbols of power and dominance, either to demonstrate conquest in areas without imperial traditions or to emphasize Inca superiority in kingdoms with them.

INCA HOUSES

Houses were similar for all social ranks: a single-roomed rectangular building with one door, often no windows and a pitched thatch roof. Walls were mortar-fitted fieldstones, mud-plastered and painted for commoners, while of finer masonry and larger for royalty, nobles and high officials.

Outside the core area around Cuzco, provincial housing was often different, of local shapes and materials (for example adobe bricks in desert and coastal regions; or round in plan and with flat, woven reed roofs). Inca policy was to leave local customs in place so long as they did not conflict with the state system. Often the only way to tell if an area was under Inca control was the presence of an Inca official *kancha* or *kallanka* among local buildings and the presence of Inca pottery.

Below: A trapezoidal doorway at imperial Ollantaytambo has the remnants of projecting stone pegs flanking the entry.

CHAPTER TWO

ANCIENT ANDEAN CITIES

Ancient Andean urbanism developed from about 500BC. Before this time, huge ceremonial centres were built to serve the religious needs of collected communities. The sheer size of many early ceremonial centres reveals the rise of leadership and the power of religious beliefs. Co-operative labour had to be organized to gather huge amounts of stone, mud for adobe bricks and mortar, wood and other perishable materials for superstructures, and fibre baskets and ropes for containing rubble core material and for hauling stone blocks into place.

The monumental architectural traditions of ancient Andean civilization preceded true cities. Once class systems had developed and cities housed rulers, priests, craftspeople and commoners, structures reflected these developments in both the elaborate palaces built near urban ritual precincts and the smaller, more squalid and irregular clusters of suburban housing in urban sprawl. Domestic architecture mostly used local materials in rough-and-ready structures, while more elite architecture brought materials from farther afield.

As petty states, kingdoms and empires waxed and waned, administrative compounds and cities incorporated vast storage structures for the collection and redistribution of wealth. Times of conflict brought social movements and the construction of hilltop forts as competition increased over valuable lands and commodities, culminating in the vast Inca Empire briefly uniting the Andean peoples.

Left: Imperial Machu Picchu in its remote mountain fastness provides an enduring image of ancient Inca civilization.

URBAN CIVILIZATION

In the Andes, urban centres evolved around early monumental architecture built as focuses of religious devotion, from about the middle of the 3rd millennium BC. Urban civilizations evolved independently in Mesopotamia, Egypt, the Indus Valley, China, Mesoamerica and the Andes. General reasons for initial urban developments are similar, but in detail the shapes of their evolution are specific to the cultural and environmental circumstances in each area.

PRE-INDUSTRIAL CITIES

The first ceremonial complexes appeared in coastal and adjacent highland valleys in the central and southern Andes by 2500BC. The earliest pattern, not truly urban, comprised stone-faced platforms with ceremonial buildings on top,

Below: Imperial Inca Pisac. Urban compounds in mountain landscapes are a constant feature of Andean urbanism.

surrounded by scattered farming and fishing villages, whose inhabitants organized the communal labour to raise the monumental structures. Their construction obviates central political powers capable of organizing and regulating the work.

None of these early sites had dense, permanent populations. They were focuses for religious devotion by the people of the surrounding communities, and had only limited residential accommodation.

Above: Andean civilization began to appear more urban from the late Initial Period onwards, here exemplified by the walled remains of Cerro Sechin.

Structures were temples and ritual courtyards, lacking the variety in shapes and sizes that indicates the social hierarchy and occupational variety characteristic of a city.

Pre-industrial urbanism is difficult to define. Scholars agree, however, that, in addition to large populations in densely concentrated residential buildings (say, more than 5,000), there must be monumental architecture, and other buildings, large and small, that serve other purposes (administration, craft production and various civic functions).

From early ceremonial complexes and surrounding towns and villages, Andean cities became large, dense urban environments. They remained the focus of religious observance, but also regulated the economy, were the centres of state manufacture and housed the political rulers. After several thousand years of evolution, Andean cities had become urban networks linked by roads, and embodied state institutions to rule empires, the ultimate culmination of which was the Inca Empire.

Public architecture represents a huge communal commitment. Even in a non-monetary economy it demands considerable resources and powers in organization and redistribution. Builders

of public architecture must be motivated and fed. At the end of 4,000 years of development, the Incas were masters at this process.

RELIGION AND ECONOMY

Two institutions governed Andean urban growth and purpose: religion and economy. These settlements were not market places (although there is some evidence of a market in Inca Cuzco); rather, they were repositories for produce, collected into storehouses by the state for communal redistribution. Supplying religious celebrants with food and drink at ceremonies linked religion and economy for a common purpose. At times of agricultural stress, stores were also used to help people through lean times.

Cities were also locations for state 'factories' – compounds in which craftspeople, supported by the state, produced elite ceramics, metalwork and textiles for royal and noble consumption.

In these ways, Andean cities fulfilled economic functions – exchange through redistribution and gift-giving – and were places of religious focus, hospitality and entertainment. Giving was reciprocal: cities were sources of gifts but also places to which to bring tax, tribute and religious offerings. Andean cities were sources of innovation and influence

Below: At royal Chan Chan, capital of Chimú, the vast city was made up of a grid plan of streets and compounds.

through these combined roles, which in turn enhanced and perpetuated their importance and power.

A specific trait of ancient Andean cities was that much of the population lived in them only part-time: urban populations rose and fell in conjunction with the ceremonial calendar. From surrounding agricultural towns and villages, and suburbs around ceremonial centres, people flocked into the great plazas for religious observances. At other times, city centres may have been largely vacant except for rulers, priests, their service personnel and elite craftspeople, watching over hundreds of empty halls and plazas.

FITTING INTO THE LANDSCAPE

Cities were part of the landscape, both physically and metaphorically. Their plans often conformed to contours – built against hillsides, terraced, set in grid plans, or sprawled across the flat desert plain incorporating natural mounds in their constructions. Principal ceremonial centres were often oriented towards specific mountains, and their profiles sometimes mimicked distant horizons. Most famously, the plan of imperial Inca Cuzco formed the shape of a crouching puma, while 4,000 years earlier, U-shaped ceremonial complexes stretched their 'arms' out to the distant rainy mountains.

The Incas often combined a dual statement – carving rooms into rocky outcrops and thus embedding their architecture in

Above: Reconstruction of the temple tomb of the imperial Lords of Moche Sipán in the Lambayeque Valley.

nature, modifying but following the landscape, at the same time emphasizing their domination of it. For example, rooms around a plaza at Chinchero mimic and complement the valley's terrace fields. At Machu Picchu, the profile of the Sacred Rock at the northern end follows that of a peak in the distance.

Tiwanaku also had a distinct imagery: it reflected Lake Titicaca, making the ceremonial core an artificial 'island' within a moat, and the Akapana platform mound simulated, in essence, the distant peak of Mount Illimani.

URBAN CONTROL

The layout of Andean cities, especially in the imperial cultures of the Wari, Tiwanaku, Chimú and Incas, controlled people's movements. Inca officials regulated access to and movement within and through public areas. Inca city plans dictated the areas and buildings to which people had access and the people with whom they interacted. Just as the land was regulated and controlled by designating different parts for the upkeep of the populace and state institutions, so cityscapes comprised buildings, streets and plazas that reflected both imperial political power and control, and also religious ideology.

CEREMONIAL CENTRES AND ENCLOSURES

Ancient Andean ceremonial architecture began with mound-building. Elevated architecture gave a structure special status, segregating it from ordinary construction: height gave spatial separation and conferred sacredness. Even the 'special' building at Archaic Period Monte Verde had a raised floor.

Mounds emulated mountains, and mound summits provided ritual spaces and platforms for sacred buildings. Ascending them was a ceremonial act, approaching the sky gods. In association with enclosed spaces, mounds were the characteristic duo of Andean ceremonial architecture.

MONTE VERDE AND NANCHOC

Andean ceremonial architecture began more than 14,000 years ago at Monte Verde in south-central Chile. Here, hunter-gatherers built a village with two groups of structures: dwellings and a special, Y-shaped building separated from them. In the latter's floor were clay-lined braziers and remains of medicinal plants, chewed leaves, seeds, hides, animal bones and apparent burnt offerings.

Truly monumental structures came several thousand years later at Nanchoc, a late Archaic Period village in the Zana Valley of north-western Peru. Between 6000 and 5500BC the inhabitants erected

Below: Interior of the Temple of Inti, Cuzco, whose niches held gold and silver figures and whose walls were allegedly lined with sheet gold.

two long parallel mounds – lozenge-shaped, c.35m (114ft) long, c.1.5m (5ft) high and 15m (49ft) apart. Each had three tiers, built over a period of time, enlarged with layers of rubble between flat tops and faced with stones.

Nanchoc's mounds established several enduring Andean architectural and religious patterns: twinned terraced platforms indicate that mound-building and the concept of duality evolved simultaneously. There was periodic construction between periods of use. Each renewal involved 'temple interment', and enlargement as the old mound became the core of the new one.

Unique among nearly 50 Archaic sites in the valley, Nanchoc was probably built by and to serve these communities. It required organized community labour. Episodic construction reveals not only sacred continuity but also enduring leadership. It was a means of reaffirming corporate identity, and twin mounds suggest early social division of kinship groups into two 'moieties'.

SETTING THE STAGE

With the stage thus set, the Preceramic and Initial periods became the platform for Andean ceremonial architecture.

Above: The Semi-Subterranean Court at Tiwanaku, a sunken enclosure adjacent to the Kalasasaya and Akapana temple mounds, is lined with carved stone trophy heads.

Ceremonial complexes became the focus of Andean architecture for the next 5,000 years throughout the western coastal valleys and Andean highlands. Some were huge; some were raised above the flat valley floors; others were terraced against hillsides. They embodied a wealth of styles and structural combinations, but always involved the formal organization of space in order to accommodate ritual and to control worshippers' access and movements.

Early ceremonial centres were nodes of religious focus among settlements, with little domestic settlement immediately around them. The same elements – platforms and enclosed spaces – became the religious precincts of later cities, surrounded by sprawling urban complexes.

Vast complexes of temple mounds and sunken court enclosures were built at Sechín Alto, Las Haldas, Huaca de los Reyes and dozens of other sites. Sechín Alto exemplifies a long, linear arrangement with a principal platform from the summit of which is a view down a succession of huge open plazas and circular sunken courts flanked by mounds. In contrast, Huaca de los Reyes comprises a large, but compact block of smaller U-shaped temple-mound groups, each embracing a rectangular sunken court, the whole itself forming a U-shaped complex with a large rectangular sunken court, beyond which is an even larger one.

THE EARLY HORIZON AND BEYOND

The multitude of U-shaped ceremonial centres that dominated the Initial Period gave way to urban centres in later periods, as political powers unified larger areas. A handful of cities began to dominate. They became the 'cathedral cities' of Andean religion and places of pilgrimage among a host of lesser sites and deities.

First Chavín de Huántar, Chiripa and Pukará introduced a new level of religious coherence in the spread of cults. Chavín feline, Staff Deity and reptilian imagery became widespread in portable and statuary art throughout the north and central Andes. The temples at Chavín de Huántar replicated the U-shaped temple formula, and introduced elements of complexity and secrecy in temple interiors previously unseen.

Below: The Pumapunku sunken court at imperial Tiwanaku, the gateway and first port of call for pilgrims to the sacred city.

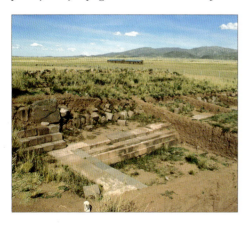

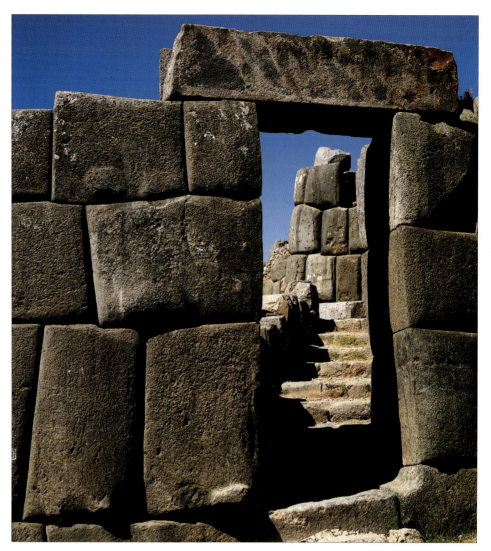

Above: One of the monumental gateways into the Sun Temple and fortress of Sacsahuaman, on the promontory north-west of imperial Cuzco.

Chiripa and Pukará, in the Titicaca Basin, developed a tradition of low mounds to support symmetrically arranged groups of single-room buildings around a sunken rectangular court. Pukará exemplifies a cult centre for double-sided Yaya-Mama (male-female) statuary that spread throughout the southern Andean Altiplano.

URBAN PRECINCTS

Cities incorporated the patterns established in these early periods. In the Early Intermediate Period, Moche and Tiwanaku brought the beginnings of state formation, with satellite administrative towns. In the southern coastal deserts, Cahuachi and Ventilla represent two aspects of administrative city and religious centre, among several forming a loose confederation.

Middle Horizon Huari and Tiwanaku were simultaneously imperial capitals and religious cities. Late Intermediate Period

Chan Chan, capital of the Chimú Kingdom, was the ultimate combination of extensive urbanism surrounding a complex of ceremonial enclosures – the enclosed cities of the dead Chimú rulers.

By the 15th and 16th centuries, Andean cities had become the focus for ceremony that symbolized the nature and existence of the state in a close alliance of religion and imperial government. Cities hosted ceremonies that were deeply imbued with meaning, ostentatious mass gatherings for festivals and the redistribution of wealth through imperial gift-giving. Precinct plans and ceremonial enclosures became imperial tools for control of both ritual and people.

RITUAL AND FUNERARY COMPOUNDS

Two ancient Andean traditions were the association of burials with temples and the establishment of cemeteries separate from residential areas. For example, Early Horizon Paracas and Early Intermediate Period Nazca cemeteries were dedicated ceremonial sites and necropolises. By contrast, Late Intermediate Period Chan Chan had cemeteries interspersed within the vast urban complex among the residential districts.

Funeral monuments were seen as a way of maintaining contact between the living and the dead. A common practice in many cultures was the periodic re-opening of tombs for the deposit of more bodies.

CEMETERIES

The most famous cemeteries are those of the Paracas and Nazca in the deserts of the southern coast. Paracas tombs show not only the characteristic Andean tradition of preserving the interred person as a mummy bundle, but also the established tradition of kinship mausoleums that became common in Andean civilization. Tombs were regularly entered to insert new burials through the generations, and the existing mummies often rearranged to honour the new occupant. There were two 'types': bottle-shaped 'Cavernas' shaft tombs, which formed a round burial chamber at the base of a shaft, with a stone-lined entrance at the top, and 'Necropolis' underground vaults of stone-walled, rectangular, upper-entry chambers, with steps leading down to stone-walled, rectangular crypts.

DEDICATORY BURIALS

Sacrifices often accompanied temple dedications. The Preceramic infant burial and sacrificed adult at Huaca de los Sacrificios at Aspero is perhaps the earliest example.

Many later temple platforms were also so honoured. Phase III at Moche Huaca del Sol, Cerro Blanco, included sacrificial burials within adobe-brick tombs, the victims laid on fibre mats within the tombs. The Phase IV mound included the burial of a man, woman and llama in a grave atop the second tier.

At Tiwanaku, headless burials were found beneath the first terrace of the Akapana temple platform. Attendants were sacrificed and interred to accompany the royal Moche burials, and one Sicán tomb at Batán Grande was accompanied by 17 sacrificial victims.

PILGRIMAGE BURIALS

The powerful oracle shrine of Pachacamac near modern Lima operated for more than 1,000 years. Its pronouncements were so honoured that even the Incas recognized its authority and sought its advice. In the Late Intermediate Period Pachacamac Ichma Kingdom, the city witnessed the establishment of numerous foreign compounds, which expanded the city.

Terraced adobe-brick platforms with ramps were surrounded within walled compounds dedicated to foreign deities. Built as elite residential compounds and sanctuaries, they included forecourts, cell-like rooms and cemeteries for pilgrims.

LINKING LIVING AND DEAD

Anticipating later Chimú practice, one mound at late Moche Galindo lies within a large, walled enclosure. With platform, storage compartments and burial mound, it may have been the residence of the city's ruling elite.

At Middle Horizon Huari, the Vegachayoq Moqo sector was first a royal palace, then 'converted' into a mortuary monument and cemetery for the deceased ruler. Parts of the royal palace were ritually interred or 'retired' – an Andean treatment of buildings as alive and needing burial.

Left: A pre-Inca burial tower or chullpa *of the Lupaka people situated at Paucartambos, near Cuzco.*

In the Monjahayoq sector, a royal tomb comprised a complex of four superimposed stone-slab burial chambers, creating a subterranean funerary 'palace'. Four rooms in the top level overlay a 21-chamber second level, then the royal tomb – a shaft and chamber forming a llama profile in plan, the entrance through the mouth and the tail forming the fourth-level tomb.

CHULLPAS AND CIUDADELAS

These practices entrenched the tradition of continuous contact between living and dead. In the late periods, burial chambers became true funerary monuments or compounds.

The Late Intermediate Period and Late Horizon Collas in the Titicaca Basin built fitted-stone towers called *chullpas*. Of volcanic masonry, circular or square in plan, one to three storeys tall, they are dressed on the exterior but left rough on the interior to form a rubble wall with beaten earth. Their interior vaults have domed tops of corbel arching, with an exterior rim projection. Access is through a small, rectangular entry at the base, facing the sunrise. Burials within are flexed and placed in a series of superimposed niches in the walls.

Erected near towns or in separated groups, the *chullpas* were family mausoleums, containing generations of burials, the bodies wrapped in rich textiles. They were regularly entered to deposit new burials or alternatively to take the mummies out to be honoured at ceremonies.

Groups of *chullpas* were erected at Sillustani and several other sites around Lake Titicaca. They are associated with standing stone circles, whose entrances also face the sunrise.

The ultimate funerary monuments are the *ciudadelas* of Chan Chan, the Chimú capital. Each high-walled enclosure was a separate 'dead' city within greater Chan Chan, and, like the palace at Huari, had progressed from existence as an imperial palace enclosure housing the royal court, to a funerary compound to house the deceased king and his retainers. Each enclosed a large plaza for ceremony,

Above: A Moche pottery model of an offering being made in a temple courtyard. Ceramic models can sometimes help us visualize how temple structures were used.

smaller interior courts and patios, housing for the king's retainers, lines of storage niches to hold royal tribute and wealth, and the royal tomb within a platform mound forming a miniature U-shaped structure. Similar Chimú enclosures were built at Tucume Viejo and Chincha La Centinela.

The Chachapoyas in the northeastern Andes built numerous cylindrical tombs at Los Pinchudos containing multiple burials.

The Inca Coricancha temple in Cuzco included special chambers to house the deceased Inca *mallquis* mummies of deceased rulers.

Left: The chullpa *burial towers of Chusaqueri, Oruro on the Bolivian Altiplano form a funerary complex for ancestor burial through generations.*

ADMINISTRATIVE ARCHITECTURE

Administrative structures are difficult to identify, but the close relationship between rulers and religious leaders suggests that some structures at early ceremonial centres were administrative.

As social hierarchy developed, higher classes gained control over disproportionate amounts of wealth, and so administrative mechanisms were needed to redistribute it. In Inca times, religious festivals provided the venue for redistribution and we can conjecture that this practice was ancient.

MOXEKE AND STORAGE

Before they could be given away, or redistributed in elite burials, goods had to be collected and stored. Rows and groups of smaller buildings around the principal religious platforms, plazas and temples were probably storehouses.

For example, the Huaca A complex at Moxeke (Pampa de los Llamas, in the Casma Valley of northern coastal Peru)

Below: Within Chan Chan's compounds were vast complexes of administrative and storage buildings around inner courtyards.

was a well-planned, symmetrical arrangement. Long corridors connected large and small rooms with wall niches, the whole forming a large walled compound – the very image of a bureaucratic structure.

Two large halls occupied the centre of the low platform, each fronted by a court reached by steps. Between the halls was an inner courtyard. To either side there were smaller rooms along corridors. In groups and lining the outer compound sides there were even smaller rooms, some with intercommunicating doorways, opening onto long corridors running the length of the compound. The complex clearly accommodated storage and public ceremony, perhaps even banquets.

Huaca A sits on one side of a large rectangular public plaza. On the other side stood a tiered pyramidal structure, with round-cornered, tower-like mounds at the rear, backing an open terrace plaza reached by a monumental staircase. The tier faces were decorated with painted clay sculptures – clearly a temple.

Similarly, the massive complex at Huaca de los Reyes, also on the north coast, comprises a principal temple platform

Above: Fine stone shaping and fitting was reserved for imperial and state architecture, as here at one of Machu Picchu's many administrative kallankas.

and plaza, plus numerous smaller groups of platforms and rows of small, single-room buildings. The vast complexes of Sechín Alto and scores of other U-shaped ceremonial centres also include numerous smaller structures around them. At these and scores of other Initial Period and Early Horizon sites, the different groups of buildings are inseparably intertwined with bureaucratic and religious activities.

It is suggested that some of the small interior rooms at Chavín de Huántar were also for storage.

DIFFERENT APPROACHES

Moche and Nazca cities represent different administrative approaches. The Moche capital at Cerro Blanco provided a model at the apex of a hierarchy of administrative structures. The two great pyramid platforms of the Huaca del Sol and the Huaca de la Luna were religious

Above: The vast mud-walled enclosed ciudadela *compounds of Chan Chan of the Chimú formed imperial cities within the city. Their carved walls shielded complexes of administrative buildings.*

monuments surrounded by smaller complexes of administrative units. Like the capital, the Moche administrative centre at Pañamarca copied many of the capital's features. A principal adobe brick pyramid platform dominated the centre of a complex of spacious courts and buildings to administer the religious and economic affairs of the region.

The Nazca confederation of states in the southern coastal deserts separated religious centres and working cities. Ventilla, a sprawling residential city whose habitation terraces and walled compounds of mounds and administrative structures covered at least 2sq km (495 acres), was linked by a road to Cahuachi, a place of religious ritual and complex of family mausoleums.

IMPERIAL ADMINISTRATION
Middle Horizon Wari developed an administrative structure that became the hallmark of the Chimú and Incas.

The modular regimentation and additive nature of Wari architecture, with rows of walled precincts and multi-storey buildings at the capital, Huari, was repeated in several provincial centres. The well-preserved grid plan of Pikillacta on Wari's southern border is perhaps the best

known. Other Wari centres were at Jincamocco, Wari's 'gateway' to the south coast, Azángaro in the centre, and Viracochapampa and Marca Huamachuco on the northern frontier.

A fundamental factor in Wari administration was a compulsion to gather and control resources – to produce, collect and store them.

Tiwanaku, Wari's rival to the south, was primarily a ceremonial centre of ritual pyramids, sunken courts and plazas, surrounded by residential areas. Unlike at Wari cities, archaeologists have found no rows of storehouses or obvious bureaucratic structures. Tiwanaku has been described as a 'patrician city', in which residency near the centre may have been restricted to aristocracy and their retainers.

CHIMÚ AND INCA
At Chan Chan, the Chimú introduced an administrative twist. Its vast compounds housed row upon row of storage rooms and niches along corridors, within high-walled compounds called *ciudadelas*. These housed the accumulated wealth of successive dead emperors. Bureaucracies of retainers continued to collect, administrate and redistribute this wealth alongside the administration of the living emperor and population.

The Incas imposed distinct administrative architecture at their provincial cities – such as Huánuca Pampa and Tambo Colorado – built to impress conquered

subjects with Inca power and authority. Although not replicas of Cuzco, they contained similar elements: a main plaza for public ceremonies (and subsidiary plazas); an *ushnu* platform in the plaza for viewing, public hearings and the administration of justice; surrounding *kallanka* compounds of buildings for bureaucratic residency and official functions; and blocks of *collca* storehouses. In addition there were temples to Viracocha and/or Inti the sun god (and sometimes to other principal Inca gods) and an *acllahuasi* compound (for the chosen women weavers and *chicha* beer makers).

Below: Tambo Colorado, so-called for its red adobe mud-brick walls, was typical of Inca provincial administrative cities, with complexes of kanchas *and storehouses.*

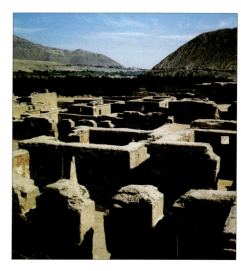

ELITE AND ROYAL RESIDENCES

Building monumental architecture involved different layers of command. There had to be leaders to marshal the labour forces, and labourers and crafts-people to do the work.

EARLY DISTINCTIONS

There is evidence of differences in residential quality as early as the Initial Period. Moxeke dwellings include some with plastered and painted interior walls and storage niches, aligned with the ceremonial centre. Most Initial Period and Early Horizon commoners, however, lived in scattered villages and farmsteads.

In Early Horizon Chavín de Huántar, only priests and special craftspeople were allowed to live near the temple.

URBAN DISTINCTIONS

This pattern prevailed into the Early Intermediate Period. With the development of cities by c.500BC, the pattern became

Below: Machu Picchu, perched above the Urubamba River north-west of Cuzco, is the best-known imperial retreat of Inca Pachacuti.

one of elite residences sited near the monumental religious precincts, with common dwellings farther out, intermixed with lesser elite residences and workshops.

At the Moche capital, Cerro Blanco, finer houses were near the base of the Huaca del Sol and south-west of the Huaca de la Luna. They were built of shaped stone and mud-plastered walls and were often painted. They had larger rooms and storage structures than the jostled, simple housing farther from the religious precinct, and their owners used finer ceramics.

Moche Galindo elite residents lived in large, bench-lined rooms, and had separate kitchens and storage rooms. Their neighbourhood was segregated from common housing by a wall and ditch. Similarly, Pampa Grande (c.AD550 to the Late Intermediate Period) had elite residences with large rooms and plastered stone walls at Huaca Forteleza, the principal pyramid, and north of it. The rich burial of the Sicán Lord with hoards of specially crafted gold, silver and other jewellery and objects reveals the existence of an affluent social class.

Above: A recessed ('double-jam') doorway at the imperial Palace of Huayna Capac at Quispihuanca in the Urubamba Valley.

TIWANAKU PALACES

Unlike earlier cities, or contemporary Wari cities, there is no evidence of blocks of storehouses at Middle Horizon Tiwanaku, or any obvious 'administrative' structures. However, from c.AD400 there were elite residential *barrios* around the ceremonial precinct. High adobe walls on cobblestone foundations surrounded elite compounds. By c.AD750 these were razed to provide space for the Putuni ritual mound–palace complex.

The Putuni ritual mound occupied a raised platform 50m (165ft) each side, with a sunken court and an eastern entrance. Adjacent, on its north-west corner, the north and west palaces were two of four palace residences surrounding a central courtyard. Each had foundations of finely cut stone and adobe walls, smoothly plastered.

The 'Palace of Multicoloured Rooms' walls were painted with blue, green, red, orange and yellow mineral pigments. Up to 15 coats of the same colour on some wall fragments reveal numerous redecorations. It had a carved stone lintel (with strutting, ray-headed feline figures), stone-paved inner patios, canals supplying it with spring water, sewage drains into the city's main drains, and a large kitchen (suitable for preparing feasts). Rooms had their own hearths and storage niches.

Right: The imperial Inca provincial capital at Huánuco Pampa in Chinchaysuyu quarter included an imperial palace entered through a wide gateway leading to a complex of kancha *compounds.*

There were dedicatory human burials at its entrance and four corners, plus a llama foetus burial. All included rich burial offerings: gold, silver, copper and stone ornaments, including a turquoise-bead necklace, gold mask or pectoral with repoussé face and other jewellery, a silver tube filled with blue pigment, a carved marine shell and finely carved bone utensils, and fine ceramics.

Other residences near the Putuni complex were also made of fine, cut-stone buildings, making the whole area west of the Akapana–Kalasasaya ceremonial precinct an elite neighbourhood.

CHIMÚ AND INCA PALACES
The compounds known as *ciudadelas* at Chan Chan were the royal residences of Chimú kings and their courts. Each comprised an elaborate complex of hundreds of large and smaller rooms, rows of storerooms and miniature U-shaped temples.

Below: The Tschudi audiencia *compound: The centre of the Chimú capital Chan Chan comprised walled royal compounds (*ciudadelas*), one for the ruling king and one for each deceased king and an attendant court and administrative staff.*

When a king died, the compound became a 'dead' palace and his tomb was bureaucratically maintained. Their massive mud-brick walls and interior walls were embellished with moulded friezes of religious imagery and geometric patterns.

Cuzco and other Inca cities, following ancient precedent, had distinct districts: *hanan* (upper) and *hurin* (lower). Although described by Spanish chroniclers as having palaces and temples around spacious plazas, it is mostly impossible to identify individual Inca structures according to function, the Coricancha temple being an obvious exception.

Inca houses were similar for all social ranks: single-roomed rectangular buildings with one door, no windows and pitched thatch roofs. Those for royalty, nobles and high officials were larger and of fine masonry.

Spanish chroniclers describe a number of palaces around the Haucaypata and Cusipata plazas in *hanan* Cuzco. The Casana compound, north-west of the plazas, comprised several large halls encircled by a fine masonry wall. Garcilasco de la Vega says that its largest hall could hold 3,000 people. Two round towers flanked the compound's main entrance.

One palace of Huáscar (thirteenth Inca emperor) was east of Cusipata, but there are no details except that it was claimed by Diego de Almagro (Pizarro's second in command), and was therefore presumably an impressive residence.

Similarly, chroniclers name other palaces at Amarucancha (Serpent Enclosure), south-east of Haucaypata, facing the Casana, which was built by Huascar and awarded to Hernando de Soto. There was also the Hatuncancha compound at the eastern corner of Haucaypata and two compounds of fine masonry halls at Pucamarca and Cusicancha, south-east of Amarucancha.

All these compounds basically comprised large halls with single entrances, built of fine-dressed masonry. It is primarily their sizes, stonework and mention by Spanish chroniclers that identifies them as 'palaces'. (Even at Machu Picchu, clearly an imperial retreat, we do not know the actual use of most of the buildings.)

Below: Fine Inca masonry is preserved in many Peruvian buildings. At Andahuaylillas, the doorway of an elite residence has a lintel carved with two facing pumas.

DOMESTIC ARCHITECTURE

Evidence of ancient Andean housing is abundant but less explored then elite and royal residences. Materials varied through time and due to local resources.

EARLY HOUSES

Hunter-gatherers used rock shelters and caves, while coastal peoples, such as the La Paloma of Chile, built reed round-houses.

Materials and styles varied considerably among Preceramic coastal villages. Huaca Prieta houses were square, semi-subterranean buildings of river cobbles, with wooden and whalebone roof beams, while houses at Asia were of fieldstones and adobe set in clay mortar. Other coastal peoples used beach cobbles, basalt and granite fieldstones, adobe or coral blocks. Many had central hearths and most had storage pits.

Highland populations lived in small, scattered hamlets and farmsteads. La Galgada is one of the few sites where houses have been excavated. They were

Below: A black polished-ware Chimú bottle shows the steep roof pitch and rectangular form changed little in the Late Intermediate Period and Late Horizon.

oval, up to 14sq m (150sq ft), with unpainted walls of fieldstones in clay mortar, earthen floors and built-in firepits.

INITIAL PERIOD HOUSES

Residential hamlets occupied hillsides and the margins of cultivable land around U-shaped ceremonial centres. Houses at Ancón and Cardál formed quadrangular groups of dwellings measuring *c.*2.5m (8–9ft) on each side. They had stone footings, but the upper walls were of perishable materials: cobbles set in seaweed and marsh grass at coastal Ancón, and fieldstones and hemispherical adobe bricks in clay mortar at inland Cardál.

Storage pits were outside dwellings, sometimes as separate buildings. Cooking was done in separate buildings or outdoors. Associated artefacts suggest that there were separate buildings for 'industry', including stone and bone working, and fibre and cotton textiles making. Early pottery serving vessels remained the same sizes throughout the Initial Period, while cooking pots became larger, suggesting increasing prosperity.

Moxeke had two dwelling groups. One, behind and aligned with the ceremonial platforms and central plaza, had houses of quarried-stone walls covered with mud plaster (sometimes painted red inside), with interior wall niches and small store-rooms behind them. The other group comprised irregularly aligned dwellings of cobblestone footings and perishable upper walls. Such differences, and associated artefacts, suggest distinct elite and common inhabitants.

At Montegrande, one of about 50 Initial Period sites in the Jequetepeque Valley, houses formed clusters around patios (inner courtyards), and were

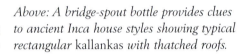

Above: A bridge-spout bottle provides clues to ancient Inca house styles showing typical rectangular kallankas *with thatched roofs.*

built of cane and mud plaster. Alignment with the ceremonial platforms indicates agreed planning.

CHAVÍN AND MOCHE HOUSING

Although Chavín de Huántar was not a city, a residential section was built in flat areas around the temple (estimated population, 2–3,000). House groups comprised fieldstone dwellings, storage buildings and workshops. Associated artefacts show that different residential clusters produced different Chavín portable objects.

Contemporary Paracas housing continued coastal traditions of single-room residences of cobbles and adobe bricks set in mortar.

From *c.*500BC Andean cities comprised central ceremonial and administrative buildings surrounded by increasingly larger suburban residential areas. As at Moxeke, social differentiation was found at Moche Cerro Blanco. Dwellings at the base of Huaca del Sol and south-west of Huaca de la Luna range from simple dwellings of river-cobble foundations and walls of perishable materials, to finer houses of shaped-stone, mud-plastered walls. The latter had larger rooms and storage structures and their occupants used finer ceramics, which were made in dedicated workshops.

Moche Galindo had four zones of residential structures, exemplifying the nature of Andean urban suburbs. Anticipating the dedicated storage blocks of Inca times, stone-lined bins were built on hillside terraces. As at Cerro Blanco there were well-built elite residences, with large, bench-lined rooms, storage rooms and kitchens, while the common, smaller houses were crowded together on the hillside overlooking the ceremonial centre, and segregated by a wall and ditch.

A similar pattern – ceremonial mound and precinct, surrounded by residential *barrios* – evolved at Pampa Grande, established *c.*AD550 and occupied into the Late Intermediate Period. There were elite residences at and north of Huaca Forteleza; high-level citizens, who oversaw the workshops, in compounds; low-level administrators in smaller compounds; and craftsmen and farmers in irregular groups of single-room residences.

Below: Rows of domestic houses formed attached 'terraces' on a regular grid plan of streets at Middle Horizon Wari Pikillacta.

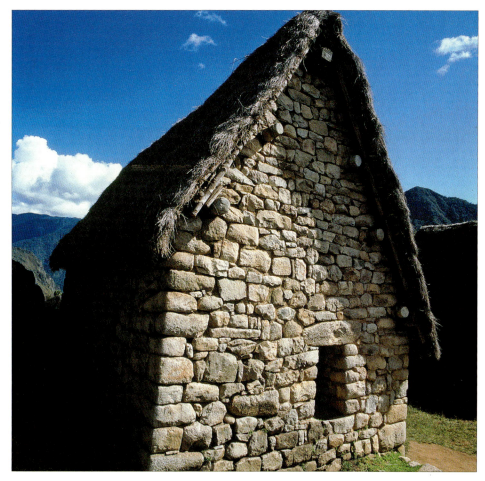

Above: The ruins of a kallanka *at Machu Picchu and the evidence from clay models enable accurate reconstruction, with a thatched roof – note the exterior stone 'pegs' on the gables, for securing the roof structure.*

WARI, TIWANAKU

Great cities of the Wari and Tiwanaku included large, suburban residential populations around their ceremonial precincts, incorporating workshops for pottery, metalwork and textiles, and *chicha* beer breweries. Wari citizens lived in rows of houses along narrow streets within large rectangular compounds. Subdividing the compounds were groups of patios (inner courtyards) with low benches and stone-lined canals, and surrounded by one-, two- or even three-storey houses (probably housing extended families), and workshops, as found, for example, at Huari, Viracochapampa, Pikillacta and other sites.

Tiwanaku citizens lived in similar housing. Distinct elite residential *barrios* at Tiwanaku were near the ceremonial plaza, while common citizens lived farther out, in cobblestone- and adobe-walled houses with thatched roofs.

CHIMÚ AND INCA

These patterns continued into the Late Intermediate Period and Late Horizon. Chan Chan's vast urban population of commoners lived around and beyond the elite residences, in *barrio* complexes of small, irregular rooms with common walls, mostly in the south, west and south-west city. Walls were mud-plastered cane or *quincha* (wattle-and-daub).

These were self-contained neighbourhoods with winding streets, common wells and cemeteries. Patio areas comprised house, kitchen, storage areas and workshops.

The typical Inca house was a single-roomed, usually single-storey rectangular structure with stone walls and a pitched thatch roof. The house was the realm of women and children (until boys were old enough to help in the fields). Inca houses were primarily shelters; most activities were done outdoors. They had only open doorways and windows. Families slept huddled together on straw or twined fibre pallets.

FORTRESSES AND WARFARE

Most ancient Andean warfare involved pitched battles on open land. Early warfare is depicted in stone sculpture and on painted ceramics. However, as periods of political cohesion interchanged with periods of fragmentation, there was need for fortifications as places of safe refuge during times of competition between city-states and in times of imperial conquest.

EARLY WARFARE

Plant and animal domestication and development of irrigation agriculture in early times entailed co-operation within communities, but as the best lands were occupied, disputes arose between communities.

The 300 carved slabs at Initial Period Cerro Sechín are a procession of triumphant warriors and their victims. Whether a war memorial for a specific victory or representing a symbolic battle,

Below: Sacsahuaman, built by Inca Pachacuti atop the hill north-west of Cuzco, had both a sacred and military function – at its core was the Temple to Inti (the Sun), while its stout stone walls and terraces formed a defensive position and its rooms were used to store military equipment.

Above: The Chimú fortress at Paramonga guarded the kingdom's borders at a mountain pass and presented a formidable obstacle to Inca conquest.

they are evidence of conflict by c.1200BC, probably small-scale, seasonal raiding between towns.

Although the Early Horizon brought religious coherence and less conflict under the influence of the Chavín and Yaya-Mama cults, sacrifice and trophy-head collection continued.

The breakdown of these cults in the Early Intermediate Period brought social withdrawal, increased competition and the abandonment of many settlements. Populations moved to hilltop fortresses

both on coasts and in highlands. Periods of drought in the early centuries AD brought hard times.

HILLFORTS

The Santa Valley and its tributaries of northern coastal Peru has been intensively surveyed, locating 54 Early Horizon sites. Most were towns – groups of small 'polities' – but 21 were hilltop forts built in remote positions to enhance defensibility. They are best interpreted as citadels, as permanent occupation would have been difficult so far away from water and agriculture. Each features one or more massive 1–2m (3–6ft) high stone enclosure walls, from which slingers could repulse enemies, plus bastions, buttresses and narrow, baffled entrances. A few have dry trenches on vulnerable sides.

Similar forts were also built in the Casma and Nepeña valleys. Chanquillo (mid-4th–2nd centuries BC), in Casma, typifies these refuges: two outer sub-circular walls with steep entrances and bastions follow the contours, encircling a lozenge-shaped inner wall. Within this are two circular towers within circular walls and a multi-roomed rectangular structure for temporary occupation.

Citadels proliferated outside the north-central coast in post-Chavín times, for example in the Viru, Moche and Chicama valleys.

MOCHE AND WARI FORTS

A typical Moche fortified site was Galindo in the Moche Valley. It began as a fortress, strategically located at the valley neck, with stout rectangular walls and parapets with piles of slingstones. It changed to a hinterland site and elite burial enclosure in the early Middle Horizon as the Moche power base shifted from south to north – abandoning Cerro Blanco for a capital at Pampa Grande, in Lambayeque.

Cerro Chepén in the northern coastal mountains is perhaps one of a chain of Moche fortresses. It sprawls across a 450m

(1,500ft) high ridge and contained a central palace with hundreds of rooms and barracks for about 5,000.

Middle Horizon Wari and Tiwanaku imperial coherence put an end to regional conflict and fortifications. Tiwanaku cities were focused on ceremony and ritual, and although the Wari conquered the central and northern Andean states, there seems to have been a guarded peace between the two empires.

The only recorded Wari fortress, Cerro Baúl (c.AD600–700), represents a brief encounter and Wari retreat within Tiwanaku territory in the Moquegua Valley. It occupies a sheer-sided mountain top of 600m (1,970ft) with 10ha (25 acres) of circular, D-shaped and rectangular single- and multi-storey structures grouped around patios.

WARRING STATES

Political fragmentation and endemic regional conflict returned in the Late Intermediate Period. Inca records transcribed by Spanish chroniclers describe intense warfare between competing 'tribes' or ethnic groups broken up into numerous petty states. Strong, warlike leaders called *sinchis*

Right: Resembling the terraced monolithic stone 'walls' at Sacsahuaman, Cuzco, the imperial Inca city and fortress at Ollantaytambo, north-west of Cuzco, could be easily defended.

built hilltop fortifications that are called *pukarás*, as is shown in the archaeological record.

The Wanka of central Peru's Mantaro Valley, for example, were typical of the Inca Fourth Age. Regional warfare caused them to build their towns on high ridges and hilltops, fortified with stout walls.

The Chimú of the north-west coast carved out the largest state. Its southern limits were guarded by the mountaintop fortress of Paramonga in the Fortaleza Valley. Massive adobe brick walls rise in several tiers to a final, central citadel-palace, with characteristic trapezoidal doorways.

As the Inca Empire expanded, it incorporated existing cities, including the Chimú Kingdom. New Inca cities served

as anchors for regional stability, rallying points, and staging points for future campaigns. These Inca administrative centres were capable of defence, but were less fortresses than imperial provincial capitals, for Inca warfare involved large armies and pitched battles. The Incas conquered by force and negotiation. Once hilltop fortresses were taken and razed they ruled through intimidation and power rather than from garrisoned citadels.

Nevertheless, Ollantaytambo in the Urubamba Valley was a combined Inca imperial retreat, temple and fortress. Built on a mountain shoulder above a strategic pass on the Inca road north of Cuzco, it was one place where the Inca court made a last-ditch stand against the Spaniards.

The fortress-temple of Sacsahuaman formed the 'head' of puma-shaped imperial Cuzco. Its circular tower was a temple to the sun god Inti and its rooms were used to store weapons and armour for the imperial troops. Its massive stone walls would have presented a formidable citadel for the capital.

U-SHAPED CEREMONIAL COMPLEXES

Sechín Alto and Moxeke-Pampa de las Llamas are two fine examples of U-shaped ceremonial centres.

SECHÍN ALTO

One of the premier examples of a coastal valley U-shaped ceremonial centre, Sechín Alto is representative of early Andean coastal religious traditions. Built and occupied from about the middle of the second millennium BC, it represents a huge investment of labour and therefore demonstrates that tremendous political power must have been used to marshal and organize the workforces needed to complete it. Its sheer size is a mark of distinction, for it dwarfs almost all other U-shaped ceremonial centres built before it or contemporary to it. Its final form

Below: Artist's reconstruction of Sechín Alto, the largest U-shaped ceremonial centre ever built, comprising a succession of plazas and temple mounds stretching c.1.5km (1 mile).

covered more than 200ha (495 acres), making it 15 times larger than the later, highland ceremonial complex of Chavín de Huántar.

The site was located and excavated by the native Peruvian archaeologist Julio C. Tello in the 1930s, and its structures were further explored and analyzed by Sheila and Thomas Pozorski in the 1980s.

Sechín Alto was built in the Sechín branch of the Casma Valley of north-central coastal Peru, south-east of the Sechín River, and was one of many U-shaped ceremonial complexes of the Initial Period and Early Horizon. The huge complex is oriented roughly north-east–south-west. Forming the base of the U shape at its western end is a truncated mound measuring 300 x 250m (984 x 820ft), rising 44m (144ft) above the floor of the valley. Huge granite stone blocks were quarried and roughly dressed to face the platform, with the blocks set in a mortar of silty clay. Later, 20th-century looters

dug a pit 20m (66ft) into the platform, revealing an inner mound made of conical adobe 'bricks' – a preceding construction of 1500BC or earlier.

Running north-east of the core mound are four large plazas: three of them are roughly rectangular and the largest is square. The three rectangular plazas each has a round sunken courtyard, aligned along the axis of the ceremonial platform. The largest circular sunken court, in the farthest plaza north-east of the base platform, is c.80m (c.265ft) in diameter. From the base platform to the most easterly plaza it is some 1,100m (3,639ft); including the base monument, the entire central complex stretches nearly 1.5km (1 mile).

Subsidiary mounds and other constructions flank the plazas along their northern and southern edges. Some are long, narrow platforms, while others are groups of aligned small square and rectangular platforms, some of which are on the tops of the long platforms. Still others appear to be complexes of rooms on the small mounds.

Farther north-west and south-east of these main structures there are scattered remains of other square and rectangular mounds, but most of the evidence for any surrounding domestic structures has been destroyed by modern agricultural activities.

Sechín Alto functioned for some 800 years, from before 1500BC to c.800BC. Its size and complexity show that it must have represented a considerable political power in the valley, which probably extended to the surrounding region, although there were four similar contemporary ceremonial centres in the Casma Valley, and five others just before the rise of Chavín de Huántar in the north-central highlands, towards the end of the Initial Period. Adjacent coastal valleys also had dozens of contemporary U-shaped ceremonial complexes.

Architecturally and religiously, Sechín Alto is considered part of a tradition called El Paraíso. It stands at the height of the U-shaped ceremonial religious creed.

Sechín Alto

Main Temple Platform

Temples and storehouses?

A, B, C, D, E successively added Ceremonial Plazas (added over a millennium of construction between c.1750 and 800 BC)

Circular Sunken Courts

Second U-shaped Ceremonial Court

Priests' quarters and storerooms?

U-shaped Ceremonial Court

A
B
C
D
E

| 0 | 100 | 200 | 300 | 400 | 500 mtrs |
| 0 | | 500 | 1000 | | 1,500 ft |

N

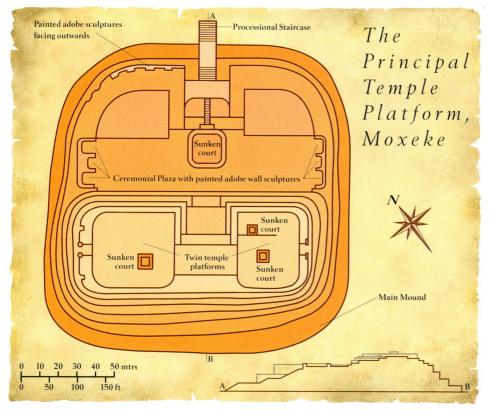

*The
Principal
Temple
Platform,
Moxeke*

Painted adobe sculptures
facing outwards

Processional Staircase

Sunken
court

Ceremonial Plaza with painted adobe wall sculptures

Sunken
court

Sunken
court

Twin temple
platforms

Sunken
court

Main Mound

N

|A

|B

A

B

0 10 20 30 40 50 mtrs
0   50   100   150 ft

Above: Plan of the principal temple mound at Moxeke, a rival centre to Sechín Alto; it formed the base of a U-shaped ceremonial complex (profile in lower right shows platform elevations from north to south).

As well as the huge base platform and wings flanking the aligned plazas, there are five 'attendant' platforms – three behind (south-west) of the main platform and two south-east of it – each forming the base of a much smaller U-shaped structure. As in all complexes of the creed of the El Paraíso tradition, the arms of the U are open to the ultimate source of the waters that make the valley fertile: the distant mountains.

MOXEKE

The contemporary complex at Moxeke-Pampa de las Llamas, south of Sechín Alto, was undoubtedly a rival. It is the second largest such centre in the valley in the later Initial Period, also occupying about 200ha (495 acres). Moxeke was first excavated by Tello in 1937.

Like Sechín Alto, it was a linear complex. At Moxeke-Pampa de las Llamas, however, there were two monumental mounds – called Moxeke and Huaca A –

separated by a kilometre of aligned plazas, the largest of which is 350m (1,150ft) long. The Moxeke tiered platform was roughly square, but with rounded corners. Atop it were several chambers, and a central staircase ascends its north-east face.

Huaca A supports a central walled compound comprising scores of small chambers, possibly for the storage of religious paraphernalia and food. Along this central plaza more than 70 rectangular stone platforms, some never completed, were erected in lines flanking the northwest and south-east sides. In some cases domestic structures appear to have been destroyed to build them, but their function remains uncertain.

The Moxeke-Pampa de las Llamas complex was built and occupied for about 400 years. Like Sechín Alto, taking the Moxeke mound as the principal platform and base of the U-shape, the open arms of the U formed by the plazas and other platforms face the north-east, to the mountains and source of life-giving waters.

Below: View of Chanquillo in the Casma Valley, once an Early Horizon fortress and probable ceremonial centre, looking towards the mountains faced by many U-shaped ceremonial structures.

PARACAS AND NAZCA CITIES

The abundance of exquisitely preserved Paracas mummy burials and their textiles has overshadowed the fact that the site was the residence of a living population as well. Archaeologists at first concentrated their efforts on what have been revealed as the dedicated cemeteries for the settlements of an entire region.

CENTRAL PARACAS
The central settlement of the Paracas people was on the Paracas Peninsula, on and around the hill of Cerro Colorado. An area of about 4,000sq m (1 acre) was occupied by habitations, known as the Cavernas phase. Square and rectangular structures of adobe walls with stone foundations were separated by narrower passageways, and compounds of such residences were scattered across the plain below Cerro Colorado. Later, the northern slope of Cerro Colorado became the new cemetery, known as the Necropolis (or Topará) phase.

Together with the deliberately separated cemeteries, the town was occupied *c*.300BC–*c*.AD200. From about 300BC

Below: The Paracas Peninsula, where three cemeteries contained generations of elite and common burials of mummified remains in multiple-layered textile bundles.

Paracas peoples were weaving not only with cotton but also with llama wool, revealing long-distance contacts with mountain herders and lending a metropolitan aspect to their culture.

TRIPARTITE 'URBANISM'
The area of the Pisco Valley and Paracas Bay is a rich environment for marine life, both on- and off-shore. Around the bay, numerous smaller, contemporary fishing hamlets were settled, whose inhabitants would have used the cemeteries as well. Similarly, in the adjacent Pisco Valley, other settlements were established for agriculture.

Altogether, domestic structures and refuse sprawl across some 54ha (133 acres). The central Paracas town was served by a spring for water, but the population relied on the settlements of the adjacent valleys for their agricultural produce.

Thus Paracas 'urban planning' appears to have comprised a tripartite pattern. Seacoast hamlets exploited the foreshore and sea, inland valley settlements irrigated and farmed the fertile lands for produce, and a central sacred town, perhaps regarded as the holiest shrine, maintained and administered sacred rites at dedicated cemeteries for the burial of the region's dead.

Above: An embroidered Paracas tunic showing a probable deity that seems to combine the Oculate Being and a Chavín-style Staff Deity, plus serpent and feline imagery.

NAZCA CONTINUITY
The partly contemporary and subsequent Nazca culture followed this pattern in the same areas of the Peruvian south coast. Nazca civilization, flourishing between *c*.100BC and *c*.AD700, was spread over a wider region of coastal valleys, making up the watersheds of the Ica and Río Grande de Nazca rivers and the Ayacucho highlands to the east.

However, in this coastal desert region many rivers never reach the sea, and in their narrow valleys support only limited irrigation networks. It has been estimated that the Nazca drainage, for example, would have been capable of supporting perhaps 15,000–22,000 people in scattered settlements.

A DELIBERATE SETTLEMENT
One of the best-known Nazca settlements is Cahuachi in the Nazca Valley, west of modern Nazca. Settlement began as a small village in the 1st century BC, and by about AD100 it had become the dominant regional centre.

Right: On the desert floor outside their cities the Nazca made and maintained hundreds of geoglyphs – ritual pathways of geometric shapes and ground images.

Its location was not accidental. For geological reasons the Nazca River flows on the surface up-valley from the site, then in mid-valley becomes subterranean, to re-surface down-valley. Cahuachi faces the Nazca Desert to the north-east, upon which the famous Nazca lines, or geoglyphs, are scattered – ritual pathways in the forms of animal and plant outlines and geometric patterns and lines.

In an area prone to drought, a need to exploit the nature of the water resource led the ancient Nazcans to develop an ingenious subterranean water-channelling system to tap the river and run-off water. Using river cobbles, they built underground aqueducts and filtering galleries, which led to reservoirs that minimized surface evaporation and fed irrigation canals. Thus the centre exploited an area of surrounding agricultural settlements and sacred landscape use.

Cahuachi comprised a core of about 40 low hills, enhanced with platforms of adobe bricks. The largest, called the Great Temple, rises *c.*30m (*c.*98ft) high in six or seven terraces. Surrounding the platforms are plazas and adobe-walled

Below: Some Nazca geoglyphs combine ritual pathways with aligned areas of large 'designated space', possibly for the gathering of crowds of worshippers.

compounds. There are no workshops or storage structures, or domestic refuse. These features support the interpretation of Cahuachi as a sacred centre, a religious city for worship and burial, which served the population in the settlements of the surrounding region. The entire settlement covers about 11.5sq km (2,841 acres).

In contrast, a nearly straight road leads north from Cahuachi to Ventilla. Here, covering at least 2sq km (495 acres; much of the site has been destroyed beneath modern agriculture), sprawled a residential city of habitation terraces, walled compounds and mounds. It is the largest Nazca settlement known, and believed to be the urban counterpart to Cahuachi.

Major construction at Cahuachi ceased *c.*AD550 as Nazca civilization began to wane.

Thus Nazca civilization, like Paracas, appears to have comprised a tripartite configuration. Dispersed settlements exploited the available coastal and valley environments, expanding on the Paracas pattern as regional population increased. Their inhabitants exchanged produce and marine resources among themselves (as well as trading with more distant cultures), and were served by specialized towns for civil administration and for sacred rites and burial. In addition, the adjacent desert floor became a canvas upon which ritual pathways supplemented the sacred purposes of the shrine and cemetery capital.

ROYAL MOCHE

The Moche people built several large man-made structures in their capital, including the alleged temples to the Sun and Moon.

SUN AND MOON PYRAMIDS

The Huacas del Sol and de la Luna formed the core of the most important ceremonial centre of the Early Intermediate Period Moche Kingdom. Construction of the two monumental platforms was begun *c.*AD100. By *c.*AD450 Moche was the capital of the southern Moche realm. Between *c.*AD300 and 550 several ceremonial centres were built to administer the southern Moche valleys: Huancaco in the Virú Valley, the misnamed Pampa de los Incas in the Santa, Pañamarca in the Nepeña, and Mocollope in the Chicama. Dominating them all was the capital at Moche in the Moche Valley.

The names 'Sol' and 'Luna' are modern. We are uncertain of the site's ancient name, but an early Spanish Colonial document refers to the site as 'Capuxaida'.

Below: Murals at Moche Huaca de la Luna include a rich array of creatures important to religious ritual and economic wellbeing – for a coastal civilization, sea fish were important.

The Moche complex follows planning traditions dating back to earlier periods in the northern and central coastal Peruvian valleys, with dominant ceremonial platforms within a working city. The two platforms stand 500m (1,650ft) apart across a now open area. The pyramids are constructed of millions of unbaked adobe bricks.

MAN-MADE MOUNTAINS

The Huaca del Sol, rising 40m (130ft) above the Moche Valley floor, is the largest single man-made structure ever built in the ancient Andes. In Andean religious tradition it appears that the Moche were attempting to create symbolic mountains on the river plain, perhaps to honour the sky gods, and in recognition that the ultimate source of the waters of their rivers came from the distant mountains to the east. Spanish treasure-seekers used those very waters in 1602 when they attempted to wash away Huaca del Sol by diverting the River Moche, obliterating about two-thirds of it. Enough of two wings remain to show the cross-shaped plan of the monumental platform.

Huaca del Sol formed a cross of thick arms on the long axis (345m/1,130ft) and stubby arms across the short axis (160m/525ft). Built in four tiers, the summit is reached by a monumental ramp up its north side.

Huaca de la Luna sits at the base of a small hill called Cerro Blanco. It was raised in three tiers against the western side of the hill to form a platform 290m (950ft) wide (north–south) and 210m

Above: San José de Moro, Jequetepeque Valley, Peru, where rich Moche tombs were found containing the remains of priestesses dressed like those in the Moche Pañamarca murals.

(690ft) deep (east–west) for the support of three smaller platform-mounds, four plazas and several roofed enclosures. It rises 32m (105ft) above the valley floor.

Below: A Moche ceramic effigy of a warrior with a war club from the Atacama Desert in northern Chile reveals Moche influence from northern coastal Peru.

Above: The huge Moche Huaca del Sol was built of an estimated 143 million adobe mud bricks. Its construction was apparently done by gangs of workmen.

Many exterior walls were whitewashed, or were painted with red or yellow ochre. The faces of many of the courtyard walls are decorated with a varied array of friezes in moulded mud-plaster and murals of religious themes. As with the Huaca del Sol, Spanish looters destroyed more than two-thirds of the uppermost tier when they dug a huge pit in the belief that the foundations contained treasure.

Archaeologists have identified eight stages in the construction of Huaca del Sol, as it was modified and enhanced over the centuries, most of them finished before AD450. At least six phases of construction are recognized for Huaca de la Luna.

NEARLY 200 MILLION BRICKS!

The millions of adobe bricks of the two pyramids themselves reveal something of the immense organizational effort necessary to build them, and the political power the monuments must represent. Archaeologists estimate that Huaca del Sol required some 143 million bricks and Huaca de la Luna 50 million. Many bricks were needed simply to bury earlier structures and make levelled platforms for new construction. The rectangular, moulded bricks are stacked in tall, column-like segments. Groups of bricks are impressed with distinct 'maker's marks', of which more than 100 marks and patterns have been found. Marks include single or multiple dots, placed at different positions on the brick faces, sometimes even in patterns resembling animal paw marks. Other marks are lines running across, down or diagonally on the brick faces. Still others are curved lines, or combinations of lines and dots. Some are miniature symbols: a dot and circle, or dot and curve; a crook-like line; an S-shape; a U-shape; a human footprint; a duck-like footprint; a dot with radiating arms; and a pottery jar profile.

A WORKING CITY

In its heyday, the ancient city covered about 3sq km (740 acres). Archaeological evidence shows that the expanse between the two platforms, and beyond them, was occupied by hundreds of workshops and houses, incorporating the religious structures within the city, much like a medieval European cathedral city. Most of the ancient city is buried beneath up to 2m (6½ ft) of washed-in alluvium.

Excavations have revealed houses; pottery, metalworking and textile workshops of cobblestone foundations, with superstructures of perishable materials (presumably cane, thatch and wood); and more well-built housing of stone, with plastered adobe walls. The latter had larger rooms and finer ceramics associated with them.

Within workshops the excavators found large ceramic water-storage jars, stores of ground clay and finished vessels, and also the kilns and tools for pottery making, including scores of moulds. Finished products included containers, many of them painted with combat and deer-hunting scenes, and figurines, portrait heads, rattles, weavers' spindle whorls and crucibles for holding molten metal. Other shops had *tuyères* (ceramic tips of blow-tubes used in metalworking) and metal slag.

Excavators also discovered a winding canal especially dug to bring water into the workshops and residential areas.

Below: A mural at Moche Huaca de la Luna shows colourful ritual imagery of Andean creatures, including humans, fish, tropical birds and monkeys, and a jaguar.

IMPERIAL TIWANAKU

The capital of the Tiwanaku Empire was the world's highest ancient city, seated on the plain south of Lake Titicaca in modern Bolivia at 3,850m (12,600ft) above sea level.

EARLY BEGINNINGS

Tiwanaku was founded as early as c.250BC, one of several centres of the Yaya-Mama religious cult, based at the cities of Pukará and Taraco at the north end of the lake, and succeeding earlier architectural traditions at Chiripa, on the south lakeshore. Monumental construction had begun by c.AD200, in the middle of the Early Intermediate Period and by AD500 Tiwanaku was the capital of a substantial empire ruling the southern Andean region through the Middle Horizon until c.AD1000. In this period of political and religious unification, Tiwanku rivalled the central Andean Wari Empire. By the Late Horizon the city lay in ruins, but was recognized as a sacred city by the Incas.

Below: A carved stone alignment atop the Akapana ceremonial mound at Tiwanaku, showing slots, shelves and holes.

At its height, the capital covered some 6sq km (1,485 acres). Notice of the ancient ruins began with Cieza de León in the 16th century. Studies of the standing monuments were undertaken by Ephraim G. Squier, Alphons Stübel and Max Uhle in the 19th century and were continued by Adolph Bandelier, who excavated several parts of the site in 1911. Wendell C. Bennett did excavations in the 1940s, as did Alan Kolata in the 1980s along with surveys of the entire region.

Excavations concentrated on the main civic-ceremonial monuments, stone gateways, ceremonial platforms and stone sculptures of the city centre, and their art. Evidence of the surrounding residential city is substantial, but much lies beneath agricultural fields. The ancient city was surrounded by raised fields created by draining the wetlands of the southern lakeshore plain with canals – a technology lost during the Spanish Colonial period but revived in the late 20th century.

THE CIVIC-CEREMONIAL CORE

Among the high Andean peaks of the Titicaca Basin, Tiwanaku was believed to be the home of mountain deities and the

Above: The so-called Gateway of the Moon at Tiwanaku, like the Gateway of the Sun, is made from a single stone block. Its lintel is carved with typical Tiwanaku geometric patterns.

ultimate origin of the Supreme Being, Viracocha. The nearby Islands of the Sun and the Moon in the southern lake were believed to be the places of the origin of celestial bodies. The ceremonial core of the city appears to have been deliberately planned as an artificial 'island', surrounded by a moat, its monuments mimicking the surrounding landscape as symbolic 'mountains' and 'valleys'.

The shape of the carefully planned ceremonial centre was conceived by c.AD300. The principal monuments are aligned east–west, and are laid out in a grid pattern. A system of stone-lined and covered drains channelled rainwater from the monuments and plazas into the moat.

Assigning exact functions to the various structures is difficult. Undoubtedly some were sacred temples and others served more civic functions, including palaces for Tiwanaku's rulers. Several monumental stone gateways into open plazas, together with standing colossal statuary, show that the core area was public and provided large spaces for ceremonial gatherings – religious and civic.

Above: The Kalasasaya walled compound and Semi-Subterranean Court in Tiwanaku's ceremonial centre reveal a huge enclosure for large numbers of worshippers and a smaller sunken court for more intimate ritual.

TEMPLES AND SUNKEN COURTS

The most sacred structure was the Akapana Temple. Standing 17m (56ft) above the city plaza, it covered an area of 50sq m (540sq ft), in the shape of a 'stepped' cross. At its summit stood a sunken court, drained by covered water channels. Its core was built up of rough fill and clay when the moat was excavated. The top is reached by staircases up the east and west ends, continuing as staircases descending into the sunken court, itself in the plan of a quadrilateral stepped cross.

North of Akapana, the Semi-Subterranean Temple (a sunken court measuring 28.5 x 26m/94 x 85ft) is entered by a staircase on its south side. From the court walls protrude carved stone heads, and in the centre stand several carved stone stelae, originally including the 'Bennett Stela' (7.3m/24ft high) of a richly dressed human, possibly a monument to one of Tiwanaku's ancient rulers. North of Akapana and west of the Semi-Subterranean Temple, the Kalasasaya is a low-lying rectangular platform (130 x 120m/427 x 394ft), which forms a large precinct for public ritual. It is reached by a stairway between two gigantic stone pillars and its walls are made up of alternating sandstone pillars and ashlar blocks.

In the north-west corner of the Kalasasaya stands the Gateway of the Sun, comprising a single huge andesite block, carved with the 'Gateway God' – a deity reminiscent of the Chavín Staff Being, standing on a stepped platform and flanked by three rows of winged figures. Within the precinct stands the Ponce Stela (3.5m/11½ft), perhaps of another of the city's rulers.

Other nearby ceremonial precincts include the Putuni and Kheri Kala compounds, aligned west of Kalasasaya, and the Chunchukala off the north-west corner. South-east of Akapana the T-shaped Pumapunku temple mound comprised three sandstone slab-covered tiers (5m/16ft high and covering 150sq m/1,615sq ft). Its sunken summit courtyard might have been an earlier location of the Gateway of the Sun.

SUBURBS OF TIWANAKU

The surrounding residential city comprised dense concentrations of adobe-walled houses on cobblestone foundations. There were also distinct elite *barrios* of high, adobe-walled compounds on river-cobble platforms. Estimates of the ancient city's population range from 20,000 to 40,000 inhabitants.

Alan Kolata describes Tiwanaku as a 'patrician city', in which residence was restricted to those who served imperial functions – a precursor of Inca Cuzco.

Below: From within the Semi-Subterranean Court the Kalasasaya's entry gate frames the Ponce Stela, one of several monolithic 'gods' standing in Tiwanaku's ceremonial centre.

IMPERIAL HUARI

Huari, the ancient Middle Horizon capital of the Wari Empire, sits in a central Andean highland plateau about 2,800m (9,180ft) above sea level. The imperial rival of Tiwanaku, together the two empires ruled the central and southern Andes, sharing much in religious heritage but differing in artistic and architectural expression, and apparently in their imperial modes of expansion and operation.

NEGLECTED RUINS

Huari's ruins were neglected in comparison to those of Tiwanaku, for they lack the obvious monumentality of singular, outstanding structures and colossal statuary. Huari's principal 20th-century surveyors and excavators are Wendell C. Bennett and Luis Lumbreras in the 1940s and 1950s, and William Isbell through the 1970s and 1980s. The ruins were noticed

Below: Cacti and agave line ancient fields near the Wari city of Ayacucho.

Above: Ruins of the hillfort on top of Cerro Baúl in the Moquegua Valley, the only valley to house both early Wari and Tiwanaku colonies.

by Cieza de León, who travelled through the area in the 1540s, though he commented only that there were 'some large and very old buildings' there 'in a state of ruin and decay'. The site has been much looted, its sculptures mostly found in nearby farmhouses and many of its walls robbed from Spanish Colonial times for building stone.

Huari did not have the ancient pedigree steeped in local cultural development that Tiwanaku did, and seems to have arisen rapidly in a region that earlier had only scattered small towns. It was a city planned according to what appear to be strict rules of modular units, incrementally expanded as need arose, but seemingly at random, without the deliberate and preconceived planning of Tiwanaku. Ancient Huari's heyday as an imperial capital was from *c.*AD600 to 800, when it covered as much as 5.5sq km (1,360 acres).

GRID PLAN

Huari is laid out across undulating terrain, disregarding local topography in favour of a uniformity of structural planning. Its architectural forms have no local or regional forerunners. It comprised a grid pattern of high-walled compounds made of roughly dressed megalithic ashlar blocks, a pattern that is the hallmark of Huari itself and of Wari provincial cities, which were built as the empire expanded.

From regional settlement, possibly as early as the 3rd century AD, the city began its rapid growth towards the end of the 5th century AD, and within 100 years had become the leading regional ceremonial and residential centre. The city grew quickly, from 1 to 2sq km (250–490 acres), until the core of ancient Huari covered up to 3sq km (740 acres), with suburban residential additions of up to another 2.5sq km (620 acres). Population estimates vary widely between 10,000 and 70,000 inhabitants.

The early city was built around several large ceremonial enclosures of dressed stone: the Cheqo Wasi enclosure, and temple complexes called Vegachayoq Moqo and Moraduchayoq. Moraduchayoq was semi-subterranean and made of finely dressed volcanic tuff blocks reminiscent

Above: This magnificent gold mask and mummy bundle from the Wari culture dates from c.AD800.

of the type of construction used at Tiwanaku, perhaps by design. Most other compound and structure walls at Huari are built of rougher, quarried stone blocks set in mud mortar.

The Moraduchayoq Temple was short-lived, however, for it was dismantled c.AD650, while more residential structures were built to fill the areas around the ceremonial enclosures. These urban and suburban dwellings were distinct rectangular and trapezoidal compounds separated by narrow streets forming a grid-like urban plan. In the northern sector of the city the compounds typically measured 150–300m (490–985ft) each side.

Within the high walls of the compounds were numerous square and rectangular courtyard groups surrounded by long, narrow, domestic rooms, some multi-storey, with narrow doorways into the courtyards and between rooms. Some compound and house walls still stand as high as 12m (40ft), indicating perhaps three storeys. Some compound walls are

massive, being several metres or yards wide. Projecting corbels supported the upper floors; roofs were probably thatched. Courtyards often had stone benches along their sides, numerous wall niches and stone-lined drains beneath their floors.

In addition to the domestic compounds, excavations revealed what must have been pottery workshops in the northern sector called Ushpa Qoto. These compounds had storage areas containing pottery moulds for producing multiple, uniform vessels and unformed lumps of clay and other pottery-making equipment.

INSTANT COLLAPSE

Much of this rapid civic expansion in Huari appears to have been unfinished. The long, massive walls, which appear to date from the city's final decades, surround compounds that were never filled in with domestic divisions, but rather reflect an ambitious urban renewal that

came to nothing. Political crisis appears to have caused the rapid collapse of the empire, for the city was abandoned shortly after the walls were erected.

Endemic of the rapid development of the capital, the Wari founded a provincial city, Pikillacta, near Cuzco, c.AD650. It comprised a huge, single rectangular enclosure 630 x 745m (2,067 x 2,444ft), enclosing nearly 0.5 sq km (124 acres). The compound was subdivided into four sectors, nearly all of which were further divided into regimented, cell-like rooms, and a few with long, peripheral galleries and halls lined with niches. There is only one larger and a few smaller open areas. Pikillacta was abandoned later than the capital, c.AD850–900. Some of the doorways were sealed and there is evidence of fire in the central sector of the city.

Below: Eroded hills tower over the stone ruins of Pikillacta, the provincial city founded by the Wari c.AD650.

CHAN CHAN OF THE CHIMÚ

The imperial capital of the Chimú Empire was founded between AD900 and 1000, and flourished until its conquest by the Incas in the 1470s. Chimú rulers were the inheritors of the north-west coast traditions of ancient Moche and Lambayeque-Sicán. Their capital, Chan Chan, was north of the river, not far from the ancient ruins of the Huacas del Sol and de la Luna in the Moche Valley.

LIVING AND DEAD CITIZENRY

Chan Chan was a city of both the living and the dead. Its centre covers 6sq km (1,480 acres), while greater ancient Chan Chan covered a total area of c.20sq km (4,940 acres). Not all of the city was occupied at the same time, and it is conjectured that city architects earmarked

Below: The central precinct of the vast city of Chan Chan, the Chimú capital, housed the compounds of the living and dead (former) rulers, and was a rich prize to the Incas.

areas of open land for future development. Nevertheless, Chan Chan at its height was the largest city ever known in the ancient Andes (and rivals the size of ancient Teotihuacán in Mesoamerica). A great wall marks the northern city limits, through which a long avenue runs north–south towards the imperial residential core of the city.

Chan Chan's most famous structures, and the ruins most examined, are its great rectangular walled compounds, called *ciudadelas* (a modern name meaning 'citadel'), enclosed within monumental mud-plastered walls. There are 10 named compounds and possibly several others recognizable in plans of the central city. Those named are: Chayhuac, Uhle, Tello, Laberinto (Labyrinth), Grán Chimú, Squier, Velarde, Bandelier, Tschudi and Rivero. All are oriented with their long axes north–south. North and east of them there are several larger structures, known as *huacas* (Huacas Obispo, las Conchas, Toledo,

Above: The Tschudi and other ciudadela *compounds at Chan Chan have hundreds of* audiencia *courtyards lined with sculpted poured-mud walls and storage niches.*

las Avispas and el Higo) – huge, presumably ceremonial, platforms, one of which (Obispo) is 20m (66ft) above the valley floor – that might have supported temples. (Treasure-seekers have so severely destroyed them with pits that we cannot be certain.)

The *ciudadela* walls are made of tapia (poured adobe or mud) on stone foundations. Most are well preserved, and stand as high as 9m (30ft). Each compound is believed to have housed the reigning Chimú emperor, along with his court retainers and civil servants to administer the affairs of state – perhaps much like the Forbidden City of imperial Chinese Beijing.

INTERIOR DIVISIONS

Most *ciudadelas* have a single entrance on the north side, through a doorway flanked by niches in which stand carved and painted wooden statues. Within, each compound is subdivided north to south, although internal organization varies in the earlier *ciudadelas*. There is first a large entry courtyard with walls decorated with mud-brick friezes, then miniature U-shaped temple structures called *audiencias* – reminiscent of the ancient U-shaped complexes of the Initial Period and Early Horizon more than 1,000 years earlier – and finally the burial platform

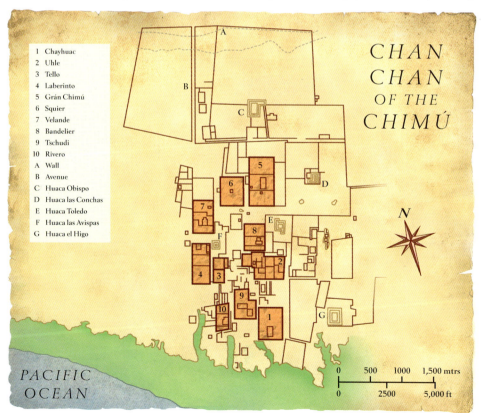

1	Chayhuac
2	Uhle
3	Tello
4	Laberinto
5	Grán Chimú
6	Squier
7	Velande
8	Bandelier
9	Tschudi
10	Rivero
A	Wall
B	Avenue
C	Huaca Obispo
D	Huaca las Conchas
E	Huaca Toledo
F	Huaca las Avispas
G	Huaca el Higo

CHAN CHAN OF THE CHIMÚ

PACIFIC OCEAN

N

| 0 | 500 | 1000 | 1,500 mtrs |
| 0 | 2500 | | 5,000 ft |

Right: The remains of a massive poured-mud wall at Chan Chan reveals the huge bulk of the royal compounds.

of the deceased ruler. Nine *ciudadelas* include a truncated pyramid in the south-east corner, concealing rooms entered from the top of the platform and a main room to house the mummified body of the deceased ruler.

Other inner courts, connected to the *audiencias*, are lined with rows of store-rooms. Adjoining wings of patios and rooms contain walk-in wells and are thought to be the residences for retainers and servants to maintain the compounds.

A CONFUSING HISTORY

The named *ciudadelas* provide a tantalizing parallel with Chimú legend. Depending on how they are designated, scholars count between 9 and 12 palace compounds. An *Anonymous History of Trujillo* of 1604 records the legendary founder of the Chimú dynasty as Chimu

Below: The poured-mud walls of every royal compound at Chan Chan are covered with sculpted geometric patterns and imagery.

Capac or Taycanamu, followed by 11 more rulers. Inca sources, however, record only ten Chimú rulers.

The sequence of *ciudadela* history is uncertain. It is argued that *ciudadela* Chayhuac, the most southerly, is the earliest, and that the capital first expanded northwards, including Uhle. Gran Chimú and the great wall demarked the northern limit of the imperial centre. Further expansion filled in the western core, including Tello and Laberinto. After that the central city was filled in with *ciudadelas* Squier, Velarde, Bandelier, Tschudi and Rivero, with room being made for the last two by razing parts of the old southern core.

Some scholars reason that the rectangular plans and tripartite internal divisions of the *ciudadelas* were inspired by the walled compounds and cell-like divisions of Wari cities. Others argue that they reflect a pattern begun in the preceding civil government of the late Moche city of Galindo, a physically much closer model.

URBAN SPRAWL

The urban sprawl of Chan Chan comprised emulative compounds of elite citizens among and around the *ciudadelas*, and compact *barrios* of small-roomed residences of the ordinary citizenry, estimated at about 26,000, in the south and west of the city. Common citizens comprised a main group of farmers, and the personal retainers of elite households, skilled artisans and craftspeople such as potters, weavers, carvers and metalworkers, traders and labourers – about half in each group.

Whereas the *ciudadelas* contained as many as 200 storerooms, no elite residence had more than 10. Ordinary citizens lived in cane-walled and plastered (called *quincha* or wattle-and-daub) houses. These had common walls and were organized into distinct *barrios* (neighbourhoods) lining winding streets. Scattered among them were a few better houses of minor elites.

Among the southern suburbs were also several cemeteries and garden plots dug into the valley floor to tap the water table (some still in use today).

THE IMPERIAL INCA CAPITAL AND ITS CITIES

The Incas established provincial administrative cities at strategic locations throughout the empire. Sometimes Inca administrative buildings, temples and ceremonial plazas with *ushnu* platforms were built within existing cities, as in the Chimú Kingdom or at Pachacamac. In other cases they built new cities, colonizing unoccupied areas by moving whole populations of conquered subjects.

CUZCO
The imperial capital, the 'navel of the world', was mostly built by Pachacuti and his successors. It had a unique plan – that of a crouching puma. Other Inca cities followed more conventional grid plans. Wedged into the confluences of the Chunchullmayo, Tullumayo and Huatanay rivers, the river courses were channelled within conduits of stone walls.

The core of the city comprised two ceremonial plazas, around which were arranged numerous *kancha* compounds of large, thatch-roofed *kallanka* halls. Some were the residences of living Inca emperors; others housed the mummies (*mallquis*) of deceased rulers.

Cuzco's most sacred building, southeast of the plazas, was the Coricancha (the 'Golden Enclosure'), the temple of the principal Inca deities: Viracocha (Creator), Inti (Sun), Quilla (Moon), Chaska-Qoylor (Venus), Illapa (Thunder and the weather) and Cuichu (Rainbow). Its masonry exemplifies Inca stone fitting and now supports the Church of Santo Domingo. From the Coricancha radiated 41 sacred *ceque* routes and lines to shrines and holy sites.

North-west of the city, the sacred temple of Sacsahuaman sat on a hill looming over the plazas and formed the head of the puma. Made of closely fitted masonry blocks and planned with regular angles to mimic the peaks and valleys of the distant mountains, its revetments terraced the summit, on which stood a rare circular Inca Sun temple. Simultaneously sacred and military, Sacsahuaman was the venue for religious ritual and the storehouse for Inca army weapons and armour.

The four main imperial trunk roads emanated from the city, leading through planned agricultural settlements, terraced fields, canals and state storehouses.

HUÁNUCO PAMPA
This imperial administrative centre was built on the highland trunk road heading north from Cuzco to Quito via Cajamarca. It sat at an elevation of 3,800m (12,500ft) in Chinchaysuyu

Above: Special niches were built into the Coricancha temple to Inti, the sun, at Cuzco, for mounting plate-gold sheets on the walls.

quarter. It was one of the largest Inca settlements, covering some 2sq km (495 acres). Construction began in the middle of the 15th century and was still underway when Pizarro invaded the empire. By then, it comprised some 4,000 structures.

Its two-tiered *ushnu* platform, symbol of Inca domination, was the largest in the empire. It measured 32 x 48m (105 x 157ft) at the base, and overlooked a ceremonial plaza of 550 x 350m (1,800 x 1,150ft).

The city contained elements similar to those at Cuzco, and fit for a major administrative capital. There was an *acllahuasi* (house of the virgins – devotees to Inti), a *kallanka* (administrative building for imperial officials) and several *kancha* compounds of administrative buildings.

Left: The rocky outcrops of Sacsahuaman to the north-west of the imperial capital were formed into the temple to the sun god Inti.

Right: Throughout their empire, along with the imperial roads system, the Incas established provincial administrative cities.

On the hillside south of the city the Incas built rows of hundreds of storehouses for goods collected by imperial tax officials.

OLLANTAYTAMBO

Like Machu Picchu, Ollantaytambo was an imperial estate and retreat north of the capital, at the confluence of the Urubamba and Patakancha rivers, in Antisuyu quarter.

The eastern part was residential, as distinct from the western side, which had a temple to Viracocha and Inti and its associated structures. Just north of Cuzco, on a spur road to Machu Picchu, it was a small city for about 1,000 permanent residents.

So close to the capital, Ollantaytambo was probably an imperial household residence, and an administrative and ceremonial centre for the empire. It was a late Inca foundation, and its Temple to Inti was still being built when the Spaniards invaded. Unused building stones, quarried from nearby Kachiqhata, litter the site.

Stone shrines at carved rock faces lie below and north of the temple hill, which is surrounded by elaborate waterworks.

Below: Huánuco Pampa, an Inca provincial administrative city, was built with mortarless, fitted stone blocks.

TAMBO COLORADO

At the end of a trunk road running west, this city linked Cuzco to the coast, near the Chinchaysuyu–Cuntisuyu border. It is the best-preserved Inca coastal foundation, deliberately planned and built in local style using adobe brick construction. Traces of red, yellow and white paint survive on the plastered walls of its *kallanka* and other administrative and residential buildings.

The city's trapezoidal-shaped ceremonial plaza has a low-lying *ushnu* at its western end.

TAMBO VIEJO

In Cuntisuyu quarter, south-west of Cuzco in the Acari Valley, Tambo Viejo was established on an ancient Nazca site. The coastal trunk road ran into its ceremonial plaza and led north to Tambo Colorado.

The rectangular plaza, built by a bluff of the river, has an *ushnu* platform of river cobbles, and overlooks the river as well as the plaza.

VILCAS HUAMÁN

As Inca imperial aspirations in the early 15th century expanded beyond the Cuzco Valley, Vilcas, 80km (50 miles) south-east of

Ayacucho in Cuntisusyu quarter, was one of the first regions conquered. The modern city covers most of the Inca buildings, but the Spanish Colonial plaza corresponds to the Inca ceremonial one. Its *ushnu* platform, on one side of the plaza, is constructed of classic Inca fine-fitted, block masonry, and is one of the most elaborate ever built. A stone staircase led to the summit through a double-jambed entryway.

Facing the plaza, the Temple to Inti sits on a triple-terraced platform with trapezoidal doorways and niches, and is approached by a dual stairway.

Below: Tambo Colorado utilized scarce local stone and the fine silts of the coastal plain to build its mud-brick walls.

MACHU PICCHU AND THE INCA TRAIL

Machu Picchu is probably the best-known and most-photographed Andean site. North of the Inca capital at Cuzco, it is perched dramatically in the high Andes above the Urubamba River, profiles of its structures framed by distant snow-capped peaks. Machu Picchu has been variously described as a remote Inca fortress, an imperial sanctuary, and a citadel – a last place of retreat and refuge of the Inca imperial household.

AN IMPERIAL ESTATE

In fact it was originally none of these things, but to some extent it effectively served in all of these capacities and more.

The site was chosen and established by the emperor Pachacuti Inca Yupanqui, the reigning Sapa Inca in the mid-15th century. Imperial and early Spanish Colonial records show that the site and area were an imperial estate of Pachacuti, subsequently inherited by his successors. Another imperial estate established by Pachacuti was at Ollantaytambo, farther upstream in the Urubamba Valley.

LOST AND FOUND

After the Spanish Conquest the site was effectively 'lost' because of its remote location. Although referred to in colonial records, its location remained a mystery and intrigued 19th-century explorers and archaeologists. It was re-discovered by

Hiram Bingham in 1911 on a general exploring expedition in which Bingham's own tale makes it seem as if he stumbled upon the ancient ruins by chance. In fact, locals had known of the site since colonial times, and a local farmer had described the site to Bingham when he and his team arrived in the valley.

Bingham brought the spectacular find to the attention of the Western world and claimed that he had discovered the last Inca capital. Subsequent systematic survey of the Urubamba Valley, however, has shown that the final Inca capital was established at Vilcabamba, much farther downstream.

Machu Picchu's inaccessible position, apparent defensive walls and surrounding dry moat led to its label as a fortress and retreat. However, its architecture is predominantly religious and these defensive

Above: Winding roads leading to Machu Picchu, probably the most evocative of all ancient Andean cities.

features appear to have been more for restricting access than for repelling attackers. A mountain road linked the site to a series of minor settlements strung up the Urubamba Valley along the forested slopes of high forest.

SACRED ARCHITECTURE

Its impressive architecture was certainly carefully built to special requirements. The granite building material was quarried locally on-site. The quality of the stone finishing and fitting is of the highest Inca standards, especially in the structures known as the Temple of the Three Windows and the Torreón (Tower; sometimes also referred to as the Observatorio). The latter was most likely actually a temple to Inti, the sun god, as indeed is perhaps the primary function of the entire site.

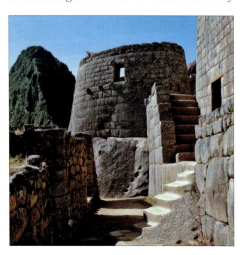

Left: The Torreón at Machu Picchu incorporates a stone outcrop with a rare Inca curved wall of fitted stones.

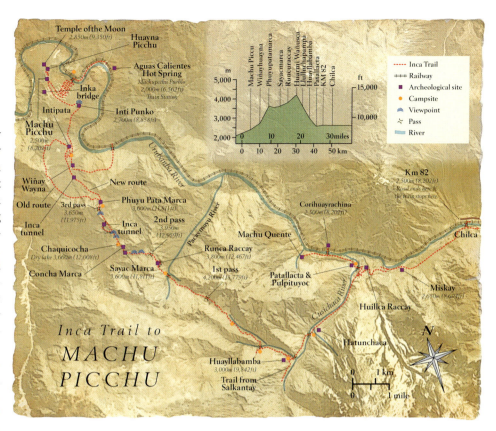

But we will probably never fully know the meaning of Machu Picchu. It is likely that the site's purpose altered through time, even though its rapid establishment and construction were planned. The Inca emperors developed a tradition of building commemorative monuments and establishing settlements to mark their conquests. Early in his reign, Pachacuti had subdued the area, in conquests that more than doubled the size of the empire ruled by his predecessor. Machu Picchu itself, together with the smaller sites and road to it (the 'Inca Trail'), are typical of such memorialization. Sixteenth-century Spanish Colonial documents of land-tenure suggest that the settlement was the headquarters of an estate founded by Pachacuti and managed through the later 15th and early 16th centuries by his lineage.

'CITY' OR MANOR?

Machu Picchu's architects integrated the structures and compounds into the lie of the land. The architecture is deliberately

Below: Machu Picchu, imperial city, estate and mountain retreat of the Incas built by Pachacuti Inca Yupanqui (1438–71).

sympathetic to Andean sacred regard for the landscape. Its dramatic structures appear 'draped' over a ridge overlooking the river. A chain of 16 spring-fed, stone-lined water channels lead into catchments to supply the site. Doorways and windows were positioned to frame views of nearby peaks of the Urubamba and Vilcabamba ranges, and natural outcrops were carved to imitate mountain shapes.

Above: The 'Inca Trail', a modern tourist contrivance, follows the route of the imperial Inca highway leading north-west of Cuzco up the Urubamba Valley to Machu Picchu.

The quality of the construction and the obvious religious purposes of many of its structures show that it was more than a remote outpost in the eastern Inca provinces, however. The residential remains at Machu Picchu indicate that about 1,000 people lived there. Together with administrative compounds and workshops it formed a functioning imperial source of income as well as a religious retreat – in fact, like many other estates, a sort of miniature city reflecting the capital at Cuzco.

BYPASSED

Machu Picchu was abandoned in the second decade of the 16th century, shortly before the Spanish invasion. It thus could never have been a last redoubt of the beleaguered Inca imperial household. The Spaniards, pursuing a rebel Inca force that had retreated to Vilcabamba, followed a route through the adjacent Amaybamba Valley to the north-east of Ollantaytambo, thus missing Machu Picchu entirely.

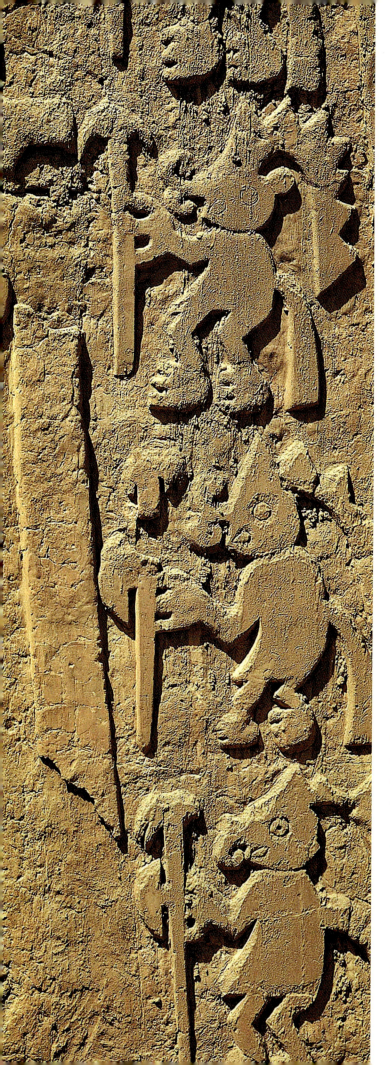

CHAPTER THREE

STONE AND CLAY SCULPTURE

Ancient Andeans sculptured in all materials – stone, clay, wood, metals and textiles. This chapter covers stone and clay sculpture.

Mountain peoples tended to sculpt in stone, while coastal peoples worked with mud and clay.

The range of styles and subjects is extraordinary. Much of the purpose of monumental stone sculpture, plaster wall carving and small clay figurines was connected with religious ritual. Whether they were made from adobe or stone, these colossal statues, sculpted walls, statuary and all kinds of imagery were carved to portray fearsome human-beast figures to awe ceremonial audiences and constantly remind them of their duties to the gods. Alternatively, statuary and imagery were buried as offerings in caches or human burials associated with temples.

Effigy vessels were especially popular from the Early Intermediate Period onwards. Almost every kind of animal and bird was sculpted. Bottles were made in the shapes of gourds. Humans are portrayed with almost every imaginable condition or doing everyday and ritual tasks.

And there are even models of buildings – curious, functional vessels in the shapes of houses and temples, which help archaeologists to understand aspects of ancient Andean life that are otherwise undocumented.

Left: Huaca del Dragón near the Chimú capital of Chan Chan – detail of rainbow and solar flare wall sculpture.

CARVING IN STONE

Stone sculpturing began in, or was brought to, the New World by the earliest hunter-gatherers. These were the carefully crafted stone tools used for hunting and food processing. Finely shaped projectile points demonstrate the developed skills of their makers as surely as do the artistic sculpted stone figures of deities, animals and plants of ancient Andean civilizations.

STONE WARRIORS

The earliest large stone sculptures of the Andean Area are the provocative incised figures on the flat stone stelae forming the wall of Cerro Sechín at the junction of the Sechín and Moxeke rivers in the Casma Valley. No other Peruvian Initial Period or Early Horizon site has more individual sculptures – nearly 400 in all.

Granite blocks quarried from the hill behind the site were carefully dressed by pecking and abrasion with sand and water to make flat-sided slabs of two sizes: $c.3 \times 1$m ($c.10 \times 3$ft) and $c.85$cm $\times 70$cm ($c.2\frac{1}{2}$ft $\times 2\frac{1}{3}$ft).

These were incised with fine lines $c.7$mm ($\frac{1}{3}$in) deep and $c.11$mm ($\frac{1}{2}$in) wide, depicting victorious warriors and their victims, plus two banners on tall stelae flanking the main platform's central staircase. Victims and their body parts – including numerous severed heads – have closed eyes and agonized mouths and are contorted in postures of torture and pain, some with spilled entrails. Marching victorious warriors carry war clubs, and severed heads dangle from their belts or hands. Two slabs with similar warriors flank the temple compound's back entrance.

The gruesome accuracy of these sculptures initiated an Andean tradition of realism in sculpture, as well as the glorification of beheading and collecting trophy heads. Similar stone slabs have also been found at Sechín Alto and Chupacoto.

Of similar date, a single, rectangular stone slab at Moxeke has two incised faces: a naturalistic human hand and a double-bodied snake.

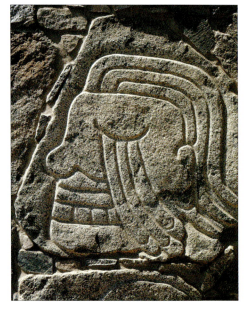

Above: Some of the earliest Andean stone carving was monumental and commemorative, including this head from Cerro Sechín.

MORTARS, BOWLS AND A MOSAIC

In a completely different style, angular mythical humanoid figures, facing full frontal (anticipating Chavín staff-bearing figures), with one arm outstretched and a corresponding motif covering one eye, adorn the outsides of large stone mortars from Santa and Nepeña valley sites.

Initial Period Cupisnique steatite stone bowls continued the trophy head motif and anticipate the complex imagery of later sculpture. Their interiors have elaborate carved spiders – an imagery anticipating Moche spider art. With bulbous bodies, exaggerated pincer-jaws, pedipalps (male reproductive organs) or spinnerets (female silk-spinning organs), they bear human faces and frequently grasp trophy heads or net bags of severed heads. They are frequently surrounded by lush plant growth, from which sprout human heads, hands and other body parts.

Left: A wall of stone slabs at Cerro Sechín shows a procession of warriors and their defeated enemies, including many body parts.

A more bizarre form of stone sculpture is the geoglyph (65 x 23m/*c.*215 x 76ft) at Pampa de Caña Cruz in the Zaña Valley. Much earlier than the Nazca lines, thousands of small rock fragments (*c.*10cm/4in in diameter) make up a rectangular face framed with 'hair', with round eyes and nose, fanged mouth and squared jaw – resembling figures on Cupisnique pottery. Two long 'legs' form a simplified body. Contrasting with the surrounding soil, dark stones outline the white stone face and body and rose-coloured stone 'hair' piece.

This 'mosaic' has no known parallel in Peru. However, large-scale religious imagery became widespread in Early Intermediate Period and later geoglyphs formed by stone outlines, especially on the Nazca desert floor.

'LIVING' STONE

The Incas are known for their precisely fitted stone walls. They regarded stone as 'alive' – indeed the Quechua word for 'boulder' also means 'to begin'.

Whereas earlier cultures carved detached monolithic and smaller stone, the Incas literally carved and modelled the landscape itself. The Observatorio or Torreón at Machu Picchu, for example, begins with the huge boulder that forms

Below: Beneath the Torreón at Machu Picchu Inca masons enlarged a natural cleft in the stone outcrop into a temple room to Inti, the sun.

its foundation, and the cleft in the base of the boulder is itself carved into a semi-hidden temple room.

Also at Machu Picchu, the Intihuatana Stone (the 'Hitching Post of the Sun') is a stone outcrop carved into angles, recesses and a central square pillar. This and other *intihuatanas*, possibly used in astronomical observations, connect the sky to the Earth in characteristic Andean duality and cosmological wholeness and containment.

The Sacred Rock at the northern end of Machu Picchu has been carefully modified into a platform 'supporting' the natural outcrop shaped to mimic the outline of the distant mountain skyline – again linking earth and sky.

The rocky outcrop at Qenqo provides another example. A semicircular enclosure forms a ritual space around a natural outcrop left untouched, as its profile resembles a seated puma. A nearby outcrop is carved into steps and water channels, while a cleft beneath them, as at Machu Picchu, is carved into a room.

The very structure of the walls at Sacsahuaman forms a sculpture in stone and space as its angles change direction to 'sculpt' the sky into light and shadow, like the distant mountains and gorges that form its backdrop. And the vast outcrop of Rodadero opposite the walls has been carved into a huge stepped 'throne'.

Above: At Sayhuite, Peru, Inca sculptors modelled a huge glacial boulder sitting on the valley floor into a miniature urban model including houses, streets, temple platforms, platforms, channels and terraced garden plots.

THREE MODELS

Among the most remarkable Andean stone sculptures are three large-scale models of Andean architecture itself.

At Tiwanaku, the Kantatayita mound east of the Akapana includes a huge boulder carved into a maquette (roughly scaled 1 to 10) of a platform and ceremonial plaza. It is complete with staircases ascending to the flat-topped platform with sunken courts, just like those of the Tiwanaku central precinct itself.

The Incas, not content to carve stone outcrops into human-scale works, carved a large glacial boulder at Sayhuite into an entire town and landscape model. In cascading terraces there are miniature buildings, patios, platforms and water channels.

Finally, above the Chinchero Valley, Inca masons carved an entire outcrop into a miniature system of terraces and enclosures, echoing the actual terraces of the valley sides. The sculpture seems both to embed the work in nature and emphasize Inca domination of the land.

STONEWORK OF THE CHAVÍN

The body of stone sculpture at Chavín de Huántar dominated the religious imagery of the Early Horizon. It comprises three huge deity idols, carved stone slabs decorating the walls of the Old and New Temple courtyards, and many smaller pieces.

STONE IDOLS

The Old Temple housed the Lanzón Stela, or Great Image, a lance-shaped granite monolith (4.5m/15ft high) carved with human, feline and serpent attributes. Its monster visage is thick-lipped, drawn in a hideous snarl and punctuated by long, outward-curving canines. Its eyebrows and hair end in serpent heads. Its right hand is raised, its left lowered, towards sky and earth deities respectively, 'embracing' the universe; its feet and hands end in claws. Its tunic, waistband and headdress are decorated with feline heads, and snakes dangle from its waist. Its notched head has a carved, cross-shaped receptacle thought to be for channelling the blood of sacrifices.

Below: The Chavín Cult's Lanzón Stela had a notch for ritual blood sacrifice and was carved with the image of the jaguar-mouthed, taloned supreme deity and serpent imagery.

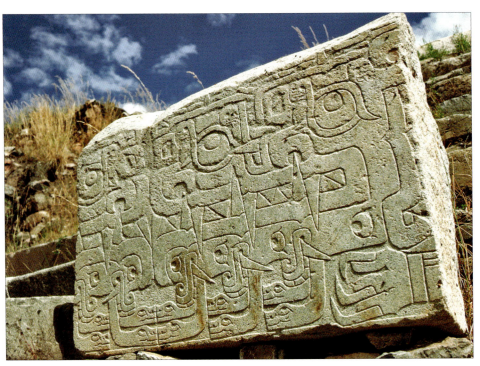

Above: Stone blocks at the entry stairway of the rectangular plaza at Chavín de Huántar embellished it with sacred cayman imagery, with rows of teeth and clawed feet, and serpents.

In the New Temple's courtyard, or perhaps in an inner gallery, stood the Tello Obelisk (2.5m/8ft high), also of granite. Its faces are carved with two jungle caymans. Notched like the Lanzón, additional carvings on and around the caymans depict plants and animals, including peanuts and manioc from the tropical lowlands, and *Strombus* and *Spondylus* shells of species native to the Ecuadorian coast, jaguars, serpents and raptors.

The Raimondi Stela, the third, and latest-dating, monolithic idol, is carved in extremely low relief on a highly polished granite slab (1.98m/6ft x 0.74m/2⅓ft x 0.17m/6½in). It depicts the supreme Chavín Cult god, the Staff Deity. Its stylistic similarity to the avian creatures on the columns of the Black and White Portal suggests that it once stood within one of the New Temple's chambers.

The Raimondi Staff Deity has clawed hands and feet, a mouth with huge curved fangs and ears bedecked with ornaments. Outstretched arms clutch elaborate plumed staffs. Unlike many other portrayals of the Staff Deity, its genitalia are non-specific, as if to embrace male and female duality and opposites at the same time, thereby balancing the Andean worldview. Further, when inverted, the image shows a new set of faces. The image appears to be rising and the eyes gaze skywards; the inverted figure's eyes look down and it appears to plunge from the sky – more duality.

In similar low relief, columns flanking the Black and White Portal depict two avian figures, heads tilted back to peer straight up, wings outspread in characteristic raptor hunting flight. The north column supports a white granite half-lintel and depicts a female eagle (identifiable by its beak cere – nostril hole – and 'vagina dentata'); the south column supports a black limestone half-lintel and depicts a hawk (identifiable by the band through its eye and a central frontal fang 'penis metaphor').

Above: The Raimondi monolith from Chavín de Huántar's New Temple was the final expression of the Chavín supreme Staff Deity.

SHAMANS AND JAGUARS

The stone walls of the sunken circular courtyard are carved with a scene of shamanic transformation. In low relief on an upper register marches a procession of profiled humanoid figures with fanged mouths and streaming, snake-headed hair. They wear serpentine belts, tunics and trousers. Their finger- and toenails are raptor claws. One carries a San Pedro cactus branch and another a conch-shell trumpet.

A lower register depicts a row of prowling jaguars on rectangular slabs. At least seven paired humanoid and jaguar sets depict a shaman in transformation from human to jaguar, using the hallucinogenic cactus in a mystic ritual.

A similar transformation is represented by fully sculpted heads on the New Temple façade. Of the 40 found, one was tenoned into the wall, revealing that the mounted set displayed a succession of 'states' in human transformation into beast. Faces alter as lips and teeth curl from human to feline fangs, snouts project, noses flatten, cheeks become scarified with whiskers and almond-shaped human eyes change to bulging round ones, weeping mucus – a reaction to drug-taking.

DUALITY IN STONE

In the Titicaca Basin, the Pukará–Yaya-Mama Cult style was contemporary with later Chavín. The hallmarks of its imagery were the depiction of yaya (male) and mama (female) figures or symbols on opposite sides of slab monoliths erected at Pukará Taraco, Tambo Cusi and other sites around the lake, and the Pukará Decapitator God. Other Pukará stone carving includes characteristic Andean feline, serpentine and fish imagery.

Writhing skyward- and earthward-facing snakes enhance the duality of the Yaya-Mama imagery. The Decapitator is a seated figure holding a sacrificial axe and severed head. With bulging eyes and feline snout and fangs, this sculpture represents the god himself or a priest wearing his mask. Many smaller Pukará figures bear female symbols of earth and water.

Portable Pukará stone sculpture included rectangular, twinned boxes, the sides depicting faces or masks surrounded with serpent and plant-like rays, anticipating the rayed heads of Tiwanaku sculpture and textiles.

Below: More than 40 jaguar-mouthed stone heads adorned the upper walls around the New Temple at Chavín de Huántar.

MONUMENTAL STONEWORK AT TIWANAKU

As an imperial capital and religious centre, everything about Tiwanaku was monumental and colossal. Titicaca was the birthplace of the world. Its city reflected the landscape; the city itself was a sculpture or model mimicking the mountains and valleys in its terraced platforms and plazas, and the rivers, lake and islands in its water channels, drains and moat.

Its statuary constantly reminded citizens and pilgrims who flocked to its temples and ceremonies of their duty to honour the gods. The Incas believed the great statues to be the ancient race of giants turned to stone by Viracocha as a flawed race.

Tiwanaku lacks Pukará occupation but inherited its sacred imagery. At least seven Yaya-Mama monoliths were found around the site, including Stela 15 (*c*.2m/*c*.7ft tall), which stood in the Semi-Subterranean Temple beside the much taller Bennett Stela. And the lower portion (the Thunderbolt) of the 2.5-tonne (ton), *c*.5.75m (*c*.19ft) Arapa Pukará monolith, which was removed 212km (132 miles) from Arapa at the north end of the lake to Tiwanaku Putuni palace.

Tiwanaku sculptors also inherited the Decapitator Cult. The black basalt image of a seated, puma-headed person (*chachapuma*) holding a severed head in his lap stood at the base of the western staircase of the Akapana platform. Another, standing, *chachapuma* also holds a severed head.

The walls of the Semi-Subterranean Temple are adorned with scores of tenoned severed heads. Unlike those at Chavín de Huántar, they do not depict shamanic transformation, but suggest that the courtyard was a place of sacrificial rituals.

SOUTHERN GIANTS

Tiwanaku sculptors carved colossal stone monoliths whose scale was unsurpassed until Inca times. The two most famous are the Bennett Stela (7.3m/24ft high) and the Ponce Stela (3.5m/11½ft high).

The Bennett Stela, the tallest Andean statue ever carved, represents a richly dressed human thought to be one of Tiahuanaco's rulers or a divine ruler. He/she holds a *kero* beaker and a staff-like object, perhaps a snuff tablet. Low-relief features portray large, sub-rectangular eyes, weeping, long, geometric-patterned streams

Above: One of several colossal monolithic stone statues in the Kalasasaya enclosed court at Tiwanaku, with hands motif.

down the cheeks, a pursed sub-rectangular mouth, and chunky fingers and toes. The massive, angular head, turban-like headpiece, belt band and short legs are reminiscent of Pukará sculpture.

Scores of small, incised figures and symbols adorn the giant's body. There are rayed faces, llamas, birds, and feline creatures and mythical beasts, snakes and panels of flowering plants – in all, some 30 figures facing frontally but with 'running' legs. The complex imagery is thought to encode Tiwanaku's state ideology and cosmology. The central rayed faces and front-facing, ray-headed figure with up-raised arms – resembling the central figure on the Gateway of the Sun – no doubt represent the creator deity Viracocha.

Left: The walls of the Semi-Subterranean Temple at Tiwanaku are lined with carved stone 'trophy' heads tenoned into the walls, possibly indicating that the sunken court was a place of ritual beheading.

Left: The Gateway of the Sun, standing at the north-west corner of the Kalasasaya enclosure at Tiwanaku has a central Staff Deity image thought by some to represent the supreme deity Viracocha.

Below: The Bennett Stela, the tallest Andean statue ever carved, is decorated with rich clothing and coca-snuff accoutrements.

Within the Kalasasaya precinct stands the Ponce Stela, perhaps another of the city's rulers, framed by the main gateway into the Semi-Subterranean Temple. Like the Bennett Stela, it portrays a richly clothed figure holding a *kero* beaker and staff or snuff tablet.

Numerous smaller stone sculptures, known as 'ancestor figures', mimic the Bennett Stela and Ponce Stela in their features and stance.

THE GREAT GATEWAY

At the north-west corner of the Kalasasaya stands the famous Gateway of the Sun. A large crack on its right side suggests that it was moved, and it is thought that it originally formed one of a series of gateways leading worshippers into the city. Several similar gateways found in the Pumapunku compound suggest that the Gateway of the Sun may once have stood there.

It is an extraordinary monolith. It appears to comprise two stone slabs supporting a carved lintel, but is in fact a single huge andesite block (3.8m/12½ft wide, 2.8m/9ft high, with a 1.4m/4½ft opening). The lintel is completely carved above its rebated jambs. The central figure portrays, in high-relief, the 'Gateway God', thought to be Viracocha the creator or Thunapa, god of thunder, a humanoid figure standing on a stepped platform that resembles the tiered mounds of the sacred precinct itself. Like other Tiwanaku imagery, he has 'weeping' eyes, an over-sized, rayed head and short legs below a serpentine belt band. Four head rays end in feline heads and the top, central ray is a front-facing feline. His outstretched arms hold staffs with raptor-headed ends. The resemblance to the Chavín Staff Deity is undeniable, but the style is definitely southern Andean. One interpretation is that the staffs are a spear-thrower and quiver of darts.

Flanking the god, in low relief, are 48 winged figures in profile (called the Tiwanaku 'angels'), in three rows of eight, running towards him. Some have human faces, others avian faces, and each holds a staff resembling one or the other of the god's staffs.

Flanking the entryway below are two rectangular niches. And the rear of the gateway has a band of three rebates to form a multiple jamb with false, blind doorways on either side and four upper niches.

Many Tiwanaku monolithic wall slabs are decorated with rows of inset stepped-diamond shapes – sometimes called the 'Andean Cross' – a shape first used in the Middle Horizon and also used on textiles and by the Incas. Numerous lintels are adorned with rows of ray-headed mythical beasts arrayed in facing lines.

PLASTER AND MUD WALL SCULPTURES

Sculptors in arid environments frequently worked in clay and mud, which did not perish as they would in the rainy highlands. This was especially true along the northern Peruvian coast in the Initial Period.

CROSSED HANDS

Kotosh, on the arid, rain-shadowed slopes of the eastern Andes, was occupied c.2500–c.2000BC. Two rubble-filled mounds supporting temples of field cobbles plastered with mud were enlarged several times. The Kotosh Tradition, probably the earliest Andean religious cult, not surprisingly also has the earliest plaster wall sculptures.

By c.2000BC the larger mound had reached a height of 13.7m (45ft), rising in three tiers and supporting groups of up to 100 successive, superimposed chambers, including seven successive temples on the lowest tier. On the middle platform, however, sat the most famous temple, the Temple of the Crossed Hands.

Below: One of the carved poured-mud walls at Huaca del Dragón near Chan Chan, showing creatures supporting a rainbow serpent and solar crescent.

Roughly square in plan (9.5 × 9.3m/31½ × 31ft), its upper walls were recessed to support a log-beam and clay-plaster roof. A painted white serpent adorns its stairway, and its entrance is red. The interior floor is split-level, with a stone-lined ritual fire pit in the centre.

The northern wall, facing the entrance, has five equal-spaced niches. The two flanking the larger central niche have low-relief sculpted clay friezes of crossed hands and forearms, one set smaller than the other. The symmetrical arrangement of niches and crossed hands are clearly early Andean expressions of duality. The different-sized hands are thought to be man and woman, signifying unity between otherwise opposing forces.

The sacredness of the temple is revealed by the fact that the friezes were carefully covered with sand before the temple was abandoned and filled with rubble.

SPIDER, INSECT AND MONSTER

Garagay, a coastal U-shaped ceremonial centre, was occupied from the mid-2nd to mid-1st millennium BC. Its Middle Temple had an entire wall carved and painted with a low-relief plaster frieze. Panels between stylized plant-like figures and geometric motifs there show three mythical creatures – humanized animals.

A face with thick-lipped, fanged mouth and languid, sinister-looking eye peers from a web-like ring. An arachnid pedipalp curls from its human nose. Farther along, a huge human-headed insect crawls along the wall, with detailed head, thorax and tail. On a third panel, an enormous split face has drooping, half-crescent eyes, thick lips and six long fangs. Traces of red, blue, yellow and white mineral paints were found on the friezes, and as many as 10 layers of clay and paint repairs.

Another wall, on the summit of Mound A, has two low-relief plaster sculptures of humans carrying round shields. The modelling of their hands and feet are especially realistic, including their nails.

Above: The Temple of the Crossed Hands at Kotosh is one of the earliest plaster wall sculptures in ancient Andean civilization. The smaller of the two pairs, crossed left over right, is thought to be female; the larger, crossed right over left, male; and together representing duality.

GODS, SHAMANS, RULERS?

The 30m (100ft), tiered rectangular platform at Moxeke was built of large conical adobe blocks and enlarged many times. The final rebuilding included massive stone revetment walls. On the third platform, large white and pink niches (3.9m/13ft wide; 1.7m/5¾ft deep), puncture the wall 10m (31½ft) above the plaza. Inside them stand colossal, high-relief unbaked clay sculptures.

Two are cloaked torsos, their heads destroyed – possibly in deliberate ritual beheadings. One holds the corners of its cape; the other wears a more elaborate cloak and twisted cord sash, and holds double-headed snakes in raised hands. Both wear short, pleated skirts. One is painted entirely black.

A third is an enormous, emerald green head with a grinning, thick-lipped mouth and rows of straight teeth. Pink vertical lines run from its squinting, half-crescent, black-pupil eyes, either side of flaring black nostrils, giving it a menacing appearance.

Above: Chan Chan surfaces were moulded like panelling and sculpted with rows of repeated animals and birds.

Another head has an expressionless face with closed mouth and eyes resembling the Cerro Sechín severed heads.

The scale, positions and appearance of these sculptures reveal a major role in ritual worship. Peering from their niches flanking the staircase, with several terraces rising behind them to a ritual platform summit, provides a dramatic, overpowering presence to worshippers crowded in the plaza below.

The Caballo Muerto mound at Huaca de los Reyes has four colossal adobe heads on its summit. Like the Moxeke sculptures, they dominate the ritual platform and the plaza below. Almost 2m (6ft) high, they portray humanoid faces with feline features: thick-lipped mouths in the same style as at Moxeke, clenched teeth, but also feline fangs, flaring, cat-like noses and huge staring, sub-rectangular eyes with deep round pupils. Like the Moxeke sculptures, they were probably once painted.

THE PUNKURÍ FRIEZES
Several successive tiers at coastal Punkurí have carved plaster friezes. The oldest one depicts a supernatural avian figure with fish and monkeys on its body.

The second platform is famous for its larger-than-life painted and carved frieze of a snarling feline on the middle of the staircase. With its green face, blue pupils, red gums, crossed white fangs and clawed

paws, it presented a startling, iconic image to priests ascending to the summit of the temple platform! Later tiers have stylized geometric forms.

A WARRIOR AND HIS CAPTIVES
The Middle Horizon Moche site Cao Viejo–El Brujo has a carved mud frieze showing continuity with the Initial Period themes described above.

Along one terrace trots a life-size warrior leading 10 naked prisoners by a rope around their necks. Like the figures of Mound A at Garagay, they show a studied realism in their movement and limb shaping. Sadly now destroyed, the top platform terrace showed the segmented

Below: The plastered walls of Moche sites, as here at the Huaca de la Luna temple, were brightly painted with geometric frames, symbols and sacred imagery.

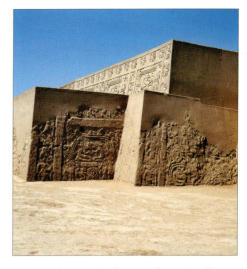

Above: The tall, thick poured-mud walls and platforms of the Huaca del Dragón (Pyramid of the Dragon), Chan Chan.

legs of a spider or crab sculpture. One claw held a sacrificial *tumi* knife, an arachnid representation of the Moche Decapitator God.

The walls at Moche Huaca de la Luna depicting the Decapitator are also sculpted low-relief plaster, but are usually described as murals because of their vibrant colours.

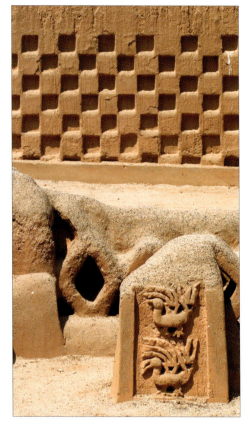

The ultimate and most vibrant expression of mud-clay sculpting is that of the Chimú in the Late Intermediate Period. Continuing early traditions of wall decorations, the Chimú covered almost every bit of wall surface in their elite residences and temples with sculptured friezes. Like Inca carving of natural stone outcrops to modify the living landscape, Chimú mud structures themselves were sculptures in their totalities.

The Kingdom of the Chimú began in the 10th century AD with the founding of their capital at Chan Chan. They were the inheritors of the Moche and conquerors of the Sicán-Lambayeque, but both continued and broke earlier traditions.

ADOBE 'MOUNTAINS'

Chan Chan was built near the mouth of the Moche River, on the north banks. The vast bulks of the ancient Moche capital's pyramids of Huaca del Sol and Huaca de la Luna, by then having stood silent for several hundred years, were only a short distance away on the south banks. They must have been regarded by the Chimú with similar awe to that of the Incas for the ruins of Tiwanaku. Like their Moche ancestors, the Chimú raised huge platforms to create 'mountains' on the flat coastal plains. Forming a crescent north-east of the city centre are four great adobe mounds supporting the city's temples: Huaca del Obispo, Huaca de las Conchas, Tres Huacas and Huaca del Higo. A fifth temple, Huaca del Olvido, lies to the south.

The most celebrated structures at Chan Chan form the vast central civic and ceremonial city core. Tall, thick walls enclose between nine and twelve huge compounds, each a city within the city, housing first the living king and then his burial mound and morbid city. The Spaniards called these compounds *ciudadelas* (citadels) because of their formidable walls and the complexity of their interior arrangements.

Above: Chan Chan of the Chimú comprises a huge ceremonial urban centre in which every surface was sculpted in mud – walls, benches, niches and pilasters.

The *ciudadela* walls are made of *tapia* (poured adobe or mud) on stone foundations. Most are well preserved, and stand as high as 9m (28¼ft). The smooth, sheer wall surfaces were rarely left unadorned, especially the walls of the huge public plazas forming the first element in each *ciudadela*.

BUILT TO IMPRESS

Perhaps inspired by the ruins of the Moche, Chimú rulers sought to impress their subjects and foreign visitors with their power. They embellished their compounds with the labours of thousands of artisans, creating a city centre that rivals the exuberance, complexity and scale of the Alhambra of Moorish Granada and the mosques of western African cities such as Djenne.

Left: Long walls at Chan Chan were moulded into panels, with sculpted channels of swimming fish and rows of part bird, part four-legged creatures.

Right: The rainbow and solar flare theme sculpted in repetitious panels at Huaca del Dragón near Chan Chan cover the entire surface of the main platform.

The chronological sequence of the *ciudadelas* has several exponents, but it is generally undisputed that they were built as each ruler died and a new ruler ascended the throne. There is some evidence that they were built in pairs. As the kingdom grew, the compounds became larger and more elaborate.

The first was probably Chayhuac, possibly that of Chimú's legendary founder King Taycanamo; then Tello and Uhle together; next were Laberinto and Grán Chimú. The late-phase *ciudadelas* – Bandelier, Valarde, Rivero and Tschudi – were built in rapid succession, the last possibly being the palace compound of Minchançaman, the Chimú king conquered by the Incas. The Squier *ciudadela* appears to be unfinished.

Below: In detail the rainbow and solar flare arch scenes differ. The enclosed figures are always the twinned mythical creatures, but the supporting figures and serpent heads vary.

PATTERN MOULDING

Using wooden moulds, the *tapia* was poured onto the walls. The clay appears to have been applied in two layers, first the poured mud wall itself, then a 2cm (¾ in) or thicker layer, which was moulded or carved while drying. There was a limited range of motifs, the Chimú preference being for repetition on a vast scale.

Repetition and angularity are used to the extreme at Chan Chan in its late phases, but at other Chimú cities, such as Huaca del Dragón, there are more rounded forms. Although there are mythical animals, in contrast to earlier traditions there is less religious imagery in preference for secular themes.

At Huaca del Dragón, a platform mound north-west of Chan Chan sometimes called the 'Temple of the Rainbow', a repeated motif features rainbow-like arcs topped with curled solar flares or wave patterns framed within moulded rectangular borders. Mythical creatures support the arc ends, themselves flanking twinned, face-to-face mythical creatures with sinuous bodies and web-like tails. Long-tailed mythical figures holding axe-bladed staffs march in a frieze above.

At Chan Chan there are panels and bands forming row upon row of repetitious geometric patterns and marching animals, birds and fishes. Vast expanses of wall are covered with diamond lattices and stepped-fret patterning. Upon closer examination of some of the latter, they are seen to be curious flying seabirds or fish. Solid bands of moulding form lines upon which march long rows of curious half-bird, half-quadruped creatures.

Huge expanses of horizontal moulded bands resemble louvred panels, bordered by rows of creatures or rows of large circular 'buttons'. The walls of many of the vast storage compounds within *ciudadelas* are formed of deep, diamond-shaped niches, almost like stacked, square-sectioned cylinders, resembling giant wine racks.

At contemporary Chincha La Centinela, the walls are carved with similar friezes of birds, fish and geometric patterns, and painted brilliant white.

CERAMIC SCULPTURE

Andean figurines were made both as solid clay objects and as functional pottery.

LITTLE IDOLS

Late Preceramic Period Aspero produced some of the earliest unbaked clay figurines, dated earlier than 2500BC. Between two floors of a temple atop Huaca de Los Idolos archaeologists found a cache of fragments representing at least 13 figurines (5–15cm/2–6in).

Eleven are women, of which four appear to be pregnant. They are seated, legs crossed, arms against their sides and forearms across their chests. Eyes and mouths are mere slits. They wear thigh-length skirts, flat hats and necklaces. A male figurine was found near by.

Below: A Nazca effigy, spouted bottle of a panpipe player, whose wide eyes and odd costume with apparently exposed genitalia indicate a religious, drug-induced trance.

Like most such items, they were produced for the public domain rather than for individual use. Similar figurines have also been found at Bandurria, El Paraíso, Kotosh and Río Seco.

TEMPLE OFFERINGS

Baked and unbaked figurines were found at Kotosh. Two crude, baked human-animal figures were associated with the Temple of the Crossed Hands, and an unbaked figure wearing a conical hat, plus three other unbaked objects, were associated with the succeeding Templo Blanco.

At Initial Period Garagay, offerings of baked and painted figures were associated with the Middle Temple and its plaster friezes. Some are dressed in minute textiles and one has fangs. Again, the public nature of these offerings and the human-beast forms of some confirm their religious connotations.

HOUSEHOLD FIGURES

In contrast, Initial Period coastal villagers produced numerous small baked solid and hollow figures of nude women, always in domestic contexts. Particular attention was given to realistic modelling of hair, facial features, breasts and navels. A larger example from Curayacu has a headband, hair falling over the shoulders, delicately fingered hands on stomach, and disproportionately short legs. The strands of hair, eyebrows, lidded eyes with pupils, triangular nose, ears and full-lipped mouth are especially finely rendered. They are thought to be associated with household curing rituals, or perhaps childbirth.

Also in domestic contexts, solid clay figurines were found exclusively in the 'elite' residences at Moxeke, suggesting the development of social hierarchy.

Ceramic figurines were relatively rare in southern cultures. One example from a Paracas burial portrays a rotund

Above: A Paracas male figurine dressed in a short tunic and mantle resembling the patterns on Paracas textiles, and a headband that appears to hold a flute.

figure with puny arms and hands on hips. A thick-necked head has a stylized face with eyes, mouth and chin rendered merely as incised lines. He wears a curious headband with circles and a tube ornament. Incised lines and cream paint indicate clothing and a bib or collar similar to actual shell and stone ones. The slit eyes may possibly indicate death, and the piece might be an ancestor idol.

Above: A mould-made Moche spouted bottle depicting a man playing panpipes, apparently very much engrossed in his music.

SEALS, ANIMALS AND TUNICS

Cupisnique peoples of the northern coast made numerous baked clay figurines and seals, both rollers and stamps (presumably for decorating pottery vessels), found in houses and graves. Examples from late occupation at Huaca Prieta include a bird stamp with a long curved beak, and a seated figurine with curious oversized hands and feet, big ears and a gnome-like hat.

Highland Pacopampa potters also made ceramic seals. One example shows a stylized feline of thick, angular, slab-like lines; there were also numerous crude animal figurines, including felines, dogs, bears and viscachas (a burrowing rodent).

In contrast, an ovoid structure, possibly a priest's residence, on El Mirador hill west of the Pacopampa temple, contained the broken remains of several fine hollow figurines. Originally *c.*48cm (19in) high, they portray tall, elegant male figures with shoulder-length hair, sideburns, unusually large ears, long, straight noses (with nostril holes) arching into eyebrows, pupil-less eyes, open, rectangular mouths, and ground-length, sleeveless tunics, but bare feet.

FUNCTIONAL FIGURINES

Later cultures made fewer clay figurines as such. The Moche and later cultures, however, excelled in making ceramic effigy vessels. Functional stirrup-spout and bridge-spout bottles, bowls and jars of all sizes and styles were made in the shapes of animals, birds and objects. There are human figurine vessels, monkey jars, jaguar bowls and deer bottles, bird vessels, vessels in the shapes of gourds, *kero* drinking cups with sculpted human faces on them, and ceramic panpipes.

A quite extraordinary Early Intermediate Period Recuay piece is of a warrior-priest in an elaborate disc and serpent headdress who is leading a sacrificial llama.

Highly polished, painted Nazca figurines of men and women are often naked except for a loin-cloth, and have tattoos or show full Nazca costume as effigy vessels.

The range of subjects depicted by Moche potters is legendary. Hundreds of Moche stirrup-spout bottles were shaped as animals and birds, and hundreds more portray human occupations and activities – everything from hunting with a

Right: A Chimú polished black-ware stirrup-spouted bottle of a dog nursing her four pups.

blowgun, warriors, flute-playing, shamans treating patients, childbirth and sexual acts of all kinds, as well as a huge range of human portrait vessels depicting all manner of human conditions and ages.

Tiwanaku and Wari, Chimú and Inca potters made jars and bowls with bird heads, humans holding oyster shells or catching lobsters, or drinking cups whose bases are shaped as human hands and feet, complete with nails.

CERAMIC MODELS

Finally, there are building models. Recuay and Moche potters, especially, made bottles shaped as houses: a Moche house with roof combs and a miniature human occupant; a Recuay court with small storehouses; a Recuay double-chambered pot with a house and man peering from beneath his gabled roof; a Lambayeque bridge-spout bottle replete with simulated stepped-fret plaster decorations and entryway flanked by two tiny human guards.

CHAPTER FOUR

CERAMICS

Most ancient Andeans used no pottery for the first 10,000 years after humans entered South America. Once ceramics were invented, however, differences in style developed rapidly among coastal and highland peoples, dictated by available materials and by cultural preferences in expression.

Fired clay, being one of the most durable materials, survives in abundance in archaeological sites. It thus forms a large proportion of the finds from excavations both as whole vessels and in fragments. It provides archaeologists with the means to recognize differences in vessel forms and decorative styles over wide areas, and through time, and thus enables them to identify cultures through their characteristic ceramics, and to determine broad themes in economic and social change and contact through trade.

Andean potters were prolific and exuberant in their output, both in quantity and in the variety of what they portrayed in natural shapes and narrative scenes painted on their pottery. These features enable scholars to surmise meanings for the repeated themes and imagery they observe, as well as to deduce the power and influence of cultures spatially and through time.

Although ancient Andeans used flat, circular potting discs from early times, they never mechanized these in any way to create a potter's wheel. Instead, they continued to make pots by the coil method, building up the vessel walls and turning the potting disc by hand merely to position the part being worked on. Other pots were mould-made.

Left: A Nazca polychrome jar, possibly for chicha *beer, depicting a warrior or entranced shaman.*

THE FIRST CONTAINERS

From the time that humans entered the South American continent, about 15,000 years ago, for more than 10,000 years they used no pottery, neither for containers nor for figurines or other artefacts. Hunter-gatherer peoples travelled light.

EARLY BEGINNINGS

Even in areas where an abundance of food and other materials allowed denser concentrations of people, ceramics came into use only thousands of years later, in the Initial Period. In these places, where the inhabitants concentrated on marine hunting and gathering, pottery would have been less useful than cotton and other fibres from gathered, and eventually domesticated, plants. Cotton was essential for nets, lines and containers for fishing.

For millennia, until knowledge of potting spread geographically, fibres and gourds were used for containers of all kinds. No doubt animal hides and wood were also used.

Examples are very few, for preservation of organic materials requires special conditions (severe desiccation or oxygen-free environments such as waterlogging), and these occur rarely in archaeological sites. However, the regular twisting,

looping and knotting techniques used to make these early artefacts indicate that before the Preceramic Period (c.3500–1800BC) there had been a long development in techniques through the Lithic or Archaic Period. No early examples include patterning or other decoration.

BASKETS AND STONE MORTARS

For the Preceramic Period there is more evidence. Sites show the gradual evolution from relatively egalitarian societies living in small villages exploiting rich resources by the sea or in mountain valleys, to the beginnings of social status divisions and the marshalling of labour for the erection of monumental architecture in complex ceremonial centres.

Excavators found twined baskets and looped reed and sedge satchels at La Galgada, in the upper Tablachaca-Santa Valley, and at Huaca Prieta in the Chicama Valley near the northern Peruvian coast, and at other highland and coastal sites. Evidence of highland–lowland trade includes bivalve shells, used as small containers for pigments.

Above: Basketry from plant fibre was also used in early containers, decorated with vegetable dyes and sometimes preserved in dry sites such as the Atacama Desert.

Stone mortars were another late Preceramic non-ceramic container found at several sites. At Salinas de Chao excavators found a large number of stone mortars used to evaporate seawater into salt crystals, for trade with highland peoples.

GOURDS

Plain and carved gourd containers, including bottles, bowls and ladles, come from a few Preceramic sites. Plain gourds were also used as fishing-net floats, and appear to have been domesticated, along with cotton, at an early date, perhaps by 5000BC. A large twined cotton fishing net with attached gourd floats was found at Huaca Prieta.

After the inner vegetable matter was removed, gourds were decorated either by excising or scraping off the gourd's outer skin when it was still soft or by incising fine lines on the surface of the gourd once it had been left to dry and harden. In a few examples a technique

Left: The earliest containers were gourds – later pottery vessels sometimes mimicked gourd shapes, as in this Chavín Early Horizon spouted bottle in the shape of linked gourds with black plant-like motifs.

called pyro-engraving was used – incising fine lines by burning and cutting simultaneously. Of 10,770 gourd fragments found at Huaca Prieta, only 13 are carved.

IMAGERY AT HUACA PRIETA

Huaca Prieta is more remarkable, however, for the discovery of some of the earliest Andean art. In addition to thousands of fragments of twined and knotted cloth found in the midden layers, two small, carved gourds were found in a burial dated *c.*2000BC or earlier.

Each is cut around the top to create a separated lid, also carved. Although the gourds are spherical, each is carved on four 'sides' with identical, repetitious patterns, with small differences. One has the same pattern, a stylized face, repeated four times. A wide, sub-rectangular mouth is slightly less wide than the two

Below: The tradition of decorating gourds did not stop after ceramics were invented. Decorated gourds at a 20th-century market in Peru mix ancient and modern motifs.

rectangular-outlined eyes with rectangular pupils. Above the eyes are angular brows, or forehead outlines, extending halfway down the edges of the eyes. Separating the faces are geometric shapes and slashes. The lid is carved symmetrically with sets of four slashes and corner triangles, forming a square, undecorated void.

Above: The earliest known decorated gourds – carved and painted – were found at Huaca Prieta, dated 2000BC or earlier.

Decoration on the second gourd comprises two images on opposing 'sides'. One image is a small, angular face similar in essential features to the faces on the first gourd, but contained in a continuous outline formed by the outer lines of the mouth and eyes. The 'foreheads' above these include varying-sized incised and excised rectangles. The other set of images appears to be stylized serpents. Each is coiled clockwise from the base of the gourd, to a blocky, stylized snake head resting above and symmetrical to the coiled tail. Two Zs and other geometric shapes are carved on the base. Most remarkably, the lid has doubled serpent, or possibly raptor, heads forming a reversed S.

The fullness of the features can only be easily appreciated when rolled out flat in a drawing, making these some of the earliest examples of hidden or obscured meaning in Andean art. They also show the early Andean liking for serpents and double imagery. The imagery on Huaca Prieta gourds and textiles resembles that on contemporary pottery from Valdivia, where ceramics were already in use.

THE INVENTION OF CERAMICS

The first Andean potters were the early farmers of the Valdivian culture of southern coastal Ecuador, on the northern fringe of the Andean Area. The Valdivian cultural area is 400km (250 miles) north of the northern Peruvian coastal Preceramic cultures, and Valdivia itself is 600km (375 miles) from Huaca Prieta. Valdivian farmers began making pottery from about 3200BC. People at Puerto Hormiga, on the Caribbean coast of Colombia, also produced early ceramics, beginning a few hundred years later, c.3000BC.

THE EARLIEST ANDEAN POTTERY
Decorative similarities on late 3rd-millennium BC Valdivian pots and contemporary Peruvian coastal gourds reveal the strength of contacts between the two regions. Shells from bivalve

Below: Two Valdivian ceramic figurines of women from coastal Ecuador, possibly representing a fertility cult.

species native to Ecuadorian waters (in particular the thorny oyster) were traded south as exotic items. Coastal Peruvians, however, found no use for ceramics at the time and preferred their tradition of gourds and fibre containers, while they imitated Valdivian artistic motifs, and may have shared the religious ideas they represented. One hypothesis suggests that the heavily wooded coasts of southern Ecuador provided fuel for firing, while the desert coasts of northern Peru did not – making the use of fired clay uneconomic.

FIGURINES
The use of clay was not altogether absent in the Peruvian coastal Preceramic Period, however. At Huaca de Los Idolos, one of the larger mounds of the Aspero complex in the Supe River mouth of central coastal Peru, excavators found a cache of at least 13 small (each only a few centimetres/inches tall) fragmentary figurines made of unbaked clay. One is a female wearing a flat-topped hat. They were buried between two floors of a room and date to before 2500BC.

Other unbaked clay figurines were found at coastal Río Seco and El Paraíso, south of Aspero, and at highland Kotosh. A few late Preceramic figurines *were* fired, indicating that the idea of hardening clay by baking was not unfamiliar south of Valdivia. It seems that late Preceramic Period Andeans preferred to fire only a few items of special significance rather than waste fuel on everyday items.

POTTERY IN THE CENTRAL ANDES
Making pottery for ordinary wares in the northern Peruvian cultures was not adopted until about 1,000 years after Valdivians began making fired pots. By about 2000BC, towards the beginning of the Initial Period, coastal and highland Andeans began producing pottery for cooking and storage containers.

Above: Some of the earliest pottery was sculpture rather than container – a Valdivian bust of a woman from coastal Ecuador.

The pots produced by Peruvian coastal and highland peoples bear little resemblance to contemporary Valdivian ceramics. Thus, although imagery on contemporary Valdivian pottery was shared on late Preceramic gourds, when Peruvian cultures began potting, their vessels were simple and the shapes imitated those of spherical, open bowl-shaped and bottle-shaped gourds.

EARLY VARIETY
From the adoption of potting by peoples of the north and central Peruvian coasts and adjacent highlands, variety developed rapidly. Vessels from the coast were limited to gourd-like shapes and had walls only 2–3mm (⅛in) thick, for example from Erizo, Ancón, La Florida and Huaca Negra. Pots from La Florida were decorated with incising, while Ancón potters decorated their pots with black paint.

In contrast, early vessels from highland sites, such as at Shillacoto, show greater sophistication and variety in shape, and a resemblance to pots from the tropical

Above: This ceramic sculpture of a Valdivian mother and child is surely indicative of fertility.

However, the introduction of pottery at Peruvian coastal and highland sites was only one part of a wider range of cultural changes identifiable, for example at late Preceramic El Paraíso. Populations at coastal sites began to shift inland, abandoning some of the U-shaped ceremonial complexes of the Preceramic Period to build new complexes in the fertile lower river valleys. As well as making pots, economics had begun to shift from marine economies to agricultural crops. La Galgada, El Paraíso, Piedra Parada and other sites show the beginning of the use of small-scale irrigation works.

There seems to be a combination of reasons for these shifts, and for the increased importance of highland sites. Population

Below: An early Chavín stirrup-spouted bottle, one of the earliest container shapes, with highly stylized feline imagery.

Above: A bizarre two-headed Valdivian female ceramic figurine, possibly representing fertility, duality, or mythological transformation.

lowlands to their east, as well as imitating some coastal features. Surface decoration on highland pots is common, especially groups of incised parallel lines and hatching, filled with red, white and yellow mineral pigments after firing. Sherds of Kotosh- and Shillacoto-style ceramics have been found at the Cave of Owls in the eastern rainforest, while tropical forest trade sherds have been found at Kotosh and Shillacoto.

NOT JUST POTS

The beginning of ceramic production is one criterion used to define the Initial Period, particularly because pottery forms an important part of the archaeological records from that point onwards, is well preserved and provides archaeologists with varieties in styles that enable them to define different cultures.

increases may be one reason, although there is no convincing evidence that coastal agriculture or marine resources were being depleted. The coincident geographic coastal uplift and ocean shelf subduction did force fish shoals farther offshore into deeper waters, and also lowered coastal water tables. Non-environmental reasons may have included competition between groups for the richest, most easily worked farmlands and simply changes in dietary and work preferences. If production of crops could be increased by moving inland to fertile lower valleys rather than risking the open sea, people may have simply made that choice from one generation to the next. The coincidence of increasingly efficient farming and the use of ceramics in which to store and cook that produce cannot be by pure chance.

THE SHAPES OF POTS

The earliest Andean ceramics were limited to a few shapes and mostly imitated the familiar forms of gourd containers. From the simple shapes of the Initial Period, however, variety soon developed into regional styles. Distinctive forms were made that became hallmarks of pre-Hispanic Andean civilization.

MAKING POTS

Ancient Andeans never invented the wheel, either for transport or for pottery making. However, fired-clay discs were used as platforms to turn vessels as they were made, the earliest known being from Paracas *c*.500BC. Interestingly, although the use of drop spindles to spin fibres was an obvious example of horizontal rotary motion, it never occurred to ancient Andeans to apply this to a spinning disc on which pots could be formed.

Andean potting used three techniques: coiling, paddle and anvil, and moulding. Coiling and hand-modelling were the principal techniques until the Early Intermediate Period, when moulding became an added method, particularly on the northwest Peruvian coast.

Coiled ceramics were made by forming long coils of clay, building up the shape of the vessels by placing the rings one on top the other, then smoothing the ridges out to form smooth sides using maize cobs, bone or wooden paddles, pebbles or shells. Cloth or hide was used to achieve a final smoothness.

The paddle and anvil technique was begun by forming the base of the vessel from a lump of clay, using the hands, or by moulding it over an existing vessel or other shape, then adding more clay to build up the sides. The sides were formed and smoothed by patting the outside with a wooden paddle, against a smooth stone held inside the vessel wall as an anvil.

Moulding involved both forming the clay over an existing form and by pressing the clay into a prepared mould (a method used particularly by the Early Intermediate Period Moche, for example). The process for smoothing the clay pot was the same as for coiled vessels.

Different cultures preferred one or other of these methods, but all three methods were employed, depending on the style and purpose of the pottery. Simple wares for everyday use were

Above: A realistic ceramic hand pottery stamp from the Early Intermediate Period Jamacoaque culture of Ecuador.

most easily made quickly by coiling, or by paddle and anvil. Such wares needed little decoration and were primarily utilitarian.

PROFESSIONAL POTTERS

Apart from such utilitarian containers, made by the users, especially in earlier periods, potting soon became a specialist's art, particularly to produce complex forms and ceramics intended for special purposes. This development coincided with specializations within society and as agricultural production became efficient enough for fewer farmers to grow enough to support full-time specialists of many kinds.

Left: Despite their zoomorphic rodent shapes, these Early Horizon Chorrera culture 'whistle' spout bottles were utilitarian.

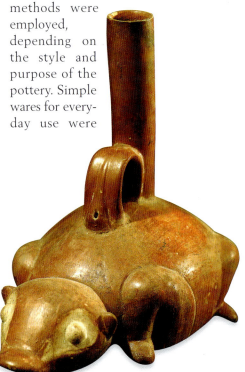

For the mass-production of vessels, an employment that became institutionalized in the great states of later periods (especially in the imperial states of the Moche, Wari, Tiwanaku, Sicán, Chimú and Inca), the use of moulds could speed up production. Nevertheless, professional potters, working full-time for the state, could also produce masses of coil-made vessels. Buildings and compounds that were pottery factories have been excavated at Wari, Chimú and Inca sites in particular. For example, Inca state potters produced uniform plates and pointed storage jars for feeding *mit'a* state workers.

TWO DISTINCT ANDEAN FORMS

Plates, shallow and spherical bowls, beakers or vases, bottle-necked jars (imitating gourds), globular jars and large storage jars were used across all Andean cultures from the later Initial Period and Early Horizon. Vessel sides and rims were straight, flared, incurved and rolled; bases were flat, rounded and in some cases had stout 'legs'.

Two distinct Andean forms were the stirrup-spout bottle and the double-spout-and-bridge bottle. The

Left: This Nazca parrot-shaped bridge-spouted bottle reveals long-distance cultural contacts.

first was a bottle with a single spout rising from a stirrup-shaped loop on the top of the vessel. The latter, as its name implies, had two spouts, between which was a handle-like bridge made from a flattened strap of plain or decorated clay. Both forms were made in a huge variety of shapes and decorations by different cultures in different periods.

Cultural styles were primarily the product of details in shape and in decoration using this range of forms.

USING POTS

The uses of pottery also quickly transcended mere utilitarian use, although that remained a principal function of form. Vessels were used for specific ceremonial roles as offerings and in the performance of ritual. Especially fine vessels were deposited in burials. And, both in life and in burial, the fineness and production quality of vessels reflected social status.

Within the range of utilitarian forms – bottles, plates, cups and jars, for pouring, eating, drinking and storage – shapes could be elaborate and even bizarre. Some pots were

Below: Another Nazca painted bridge-spouted bottle, of more 'conventional' container shape, depicts strange humanoid figures seemingly participating in drug-induced trances or transformation ceremonies.

undoubtedly purely ornamental – perhaps a household prized possession, or made specifically for burial.

EFFIGIES AND BIZARRE FORMS

Many ceramic pieces, especially stirrup-spout and double-spout-and-bridge bottles, and beakers/vases, were made as effigy vessels. They depicted either individuals as types within society (for example a shaman) or an actual individual (a practice possibly unique among the Moche). Bottles and other containers were made in the shapes of animals (for example for incense burning in a bowl forming the animal's body). Others imitated vegetable shapes, such as gourds, tubers and cactuses. Some bottle bodies were even rectangular-sided and stepped.

Still other vessels, perfectly functional, depicted whole scenes, such as a shaman healing a patient, priestly animalistic transformation, coca snuffing, combat and sexual acts. Moche ceramics are especially notable for such moulded imagery, while Nazca and other styles are especially notable for depicting such themes as painted decoration.

Fired ceramics were also used for other artefacts. Figurines were produced in abundance probably as votive offerings at temples and to represent deities. There were also ceramic masks depicting deities. Models of temples, houses and storehouses were made, and even fired clay panpipes.

CERAMIC DECORATION

Just as there was great variation in the details of shapes among the primary ceramic vessel forms in Andean civilization, so also were there a number of decorative techniques. Variation in the use of these produced distinctive styles among cultures and through time. The imagery and geometric or abstract decoration of Andean pots was done using all these methods, and by combinations of them.

POLISHING

Glazing was unknown in pre-Hispanic America, but a fine shine could be achieved by polishing the surface with a fine, hard stone, and by rubbing the partially dried pot with the hands or a cloth before firing. Moche potters polished the painted areas of their pots, while Nazca potters carefully polished the whole design area, sometimes smudging the paint colours. Early Horizon Chavín and Late Intermediate Period Chimú potters produced distinctive, highly polished, shiny black wares.

MODELLING, TWO-PART MOULDS AND CUT DECORATION

Modelling was accomplished by making the desired shape by hand moulding, building up the object, animal, plant or person in bits. Wooden and bone sticks and punches, and metal tools and knives were also used to achieve finer shaping. From the Early Intermediate Period onwards the use of fired-clay moulds in two halves became widespread, especially among north-west coast cultures.

If the vessel was not moulded, decorative techniques applied to the smoothed surface included punching, incising, excising, stamping and painting. Punched and incised decorations were some of the earliest techniques. Rows of punched dots, incised lines (cutting into the surface with a sharp tool) and shapes were used extensively on Initial Period ceramics among the coastal and inland cultures whose

peoples built U-shaped ceremonial centres. Excision (cutting out fine sections of clay from the pot's surface, leaving a recessed area) was also was used to make symbolic images and geometric designs.

SLIPS AND PAINTING

Pigments derived from vegetables and ground minerals were used to make paints and thick pastes to rub into incised and excised decorations. Runny 'paint' (a suspension of fine clay in water) was also used as slips to cover a vessel surface or chosen areas.

The earliest paints were used in the 2nd millennium BC in pottery from Kotosh, Shillacoto and other highland sites, whose potters applied red, white and yellow paint to rows of incised lines

Above: An Early Intermediate Period Tuncahuan bowl from Ecuador with geometric decoration.

and patterns. In the 1st millennium BC, potters in southern Peru began to apply mineral pigments mixed with plant resins into incised designs, after firing, to form a lacquer-like coating. Such post-firing painting and use of resin became a distinctive practice among Paracas potters.

Slips were usually applied by dipping the vessel in the paint. Areas that a potter wanted to remain free of colour were protected by the use of wax. After dipping, the wax was melted away to reveal the, usually lighter, clay colour, creating a negative painted effect. Paracas and Nazca potters were particularly fond of this method.

Paint colours included white, black, brown, red, yellow, purple and blue; variations in shades and intensity produced grey, orange, pink and violet. The Nazca used up to 15 distinct colours. Pigment sources probably included haematite (iron ore) for red, limonite (hydrated haematite) for yellow and possibly manganese and pyrolusite (magnesium dioxide) as sources of black.

In contrast, Moche potters used mainly red and white slips, both made from fine white and red clay, the latter being the same clay from which the Moche made their pots. Black and red were also used for fine-line drawing of narrative scenes, depicting everything from ceremonial sacrifice and ritual combat to hunting scenes. Often, both unpainted and painted areas were polished to create different shades of red and white to cream.

As well as rubbing paints and pastes into incised and excised areas, and negative painting techniques, paints were probably applied with fine animal-hair or vegetable-fibre brushes.

STAMPING

Another method of decoration was the use of stamps and pressing a negative moulded figure on to the vessel surface (as opposed to moulding the entire vessel using two half moulds). Combinations of lines and geometric patterns were made by pressing a wooden paddle stamp on to the wet pot to raise the design above the vessel's wall. Fired-clay stamps were also used to raise geometric, floral and animal designs and figures.

Left: A terracotta model of a house from the Cupisnique culture, c.700–300BC. Many such pieces were highly polished.

Above: A double-bodied, spouted Chancay bottle from the Late Intermediate Period possibly implies duality by its half-and-half painted body.

COMBINING TECHNIQUES

Nazca, Moche, Wari and Tiwanaku potters, in particular, excelled in combinations of all sorts of moulded and modelled, then painted, effigy vessels.

The potters made and depicted many kinds of people, deities, animals and plants. There are vessels showing single figures and groups of figures, young and old, performing all manner of daily tasks, from hunting, combat, sacrifice and ceremony, to washing one's hair, expressing the pain of a backache, giving birth or having sex.

Occasionally, shell and stone (e.g. turquoise) inlays were also applied to decorate pottery, for example as eyes.

CULTURAL STYLES

Cultural styles were mainly distinct in details of shape within a range of vessel forms, and in their methods and types of decorations applied to them.

INITIAL COASTAL AND HIGHLAND

After introduction *c.*2000BC, Andean ceramic styles began differentiating within coastal and highland cultures. North and central coastal potters used simple designs of incised lines and geometric shapes. Virú and Moche valley potters, by contrast, made thick-walled, dark red and black bowls and necked jars, mainly plain, but also with simple finger impressions, punched and incised patterns.

The central coastal Ancón style featured similar forms with incised and punched decoration, sometimes painted. Pottery making had reached south coastal sites by *c.*1300BC, where its most distinguishing characteristic

was the use of negative painting (masking areas before dipping the pot into slip paint).

The highland Wairajirca style – at Kotosh, Shillacoto and other sites – developed from *c.*1800BC. The most common forms were cups, bowls and vases, but the first stirrup-spout bottles were also made. Decoration comprised bands of incised lines and circles filled with red, white and yellow paints after firing. Raised patterns were created by excision. Highland styles show similarities to contemporary eastern tropical lowland Tutishcainyo ceramics.

EARLY HORIZON STYLES

Three distinctive Early Horizon styles were Chavín culture in the highlands, Cupisnique on the north-west coast and Paracas on the south coast. Chavín potters made distinctive polished grey-black ware – open bowls, globular and stirrup-spout bottles. Decoration was mostly incising, but also stamping and punching. Contrasting areas were defined by polishing and texturing with depressions by shells or combs and also by applying dark red and graphite grey paints. More complex geometric patterns and symbolic serpent, feline and bird imagery came later.

Cupisnique-style bottles and globular vessels are typically black or grey. Stirrup-spout bottles feature a trapezoidal-shaped stirrup, including effigy vessels of marine and terrestrial animals and people. Irregular incised lines were sometimes filled with red paint after firing.

Early Paracas potters produced Chavín-inspired stirrup-spout bottles and forms with fine-line incised feline imagery. In

Left: An Inca effigy jar portraying a man carrying a jug and kero *cups, probably for* chicha *beer for ritual drinking, and wearing a half-moon pendant.*

Above: An Early Intermediate Period Virú bridge-spouted, double-bodied bottle, possibly a whistle vessel, with a parrot head.

the later 1st millennium BC, the Paracas style developed distinctive, highly colourful ceramics using incised patterns and imagery filled with red, orange, yellow, blue, green and brown paints and resin after firing. Circle, dot and line patterns were used to create a negative painted effect in lighter slip-colour under a dark over-colour.

EARLY INTERMEDIATE PERIOD

Prominent styles in the Early Intermediate Period were dominated by north-west coastal Salinar, Gallinazo, Recuay and Moche wares and by south coastal Nazca and early Tiwanaku pottery. The quality and quantity of production indicates that potters had become full-time specialists, perhaps supported by the state. Mould-made ceramics became dominant in the north, while coil-made and highly colourful pottery characterized southern styles.

Salinar potters introduced the double-spout-and-bridge bottle. Use of Chavín-Cupisnique feline motifs waned, while human and animal effigy vessels proliferated, including erotic imagery. Gallinazo ceramics shared and continued these features with highly naturalistic modelling and introduced negative painting techniques on geometric and feline imagery.

Contemporary Moche coastal and adjacent highland Recuay styles introduced an exuberance of modelled and moulded effigy forms representing all manner of life scenes from the exotic to the mundane, including human portraiture. Utilitarian forms included bowls, bottles, jars, dippers and spoons. Moche pottery is distinctive for its highly polished, bright red colour, and for its depiction of narrative scenes in fine red or black line drawings. It has been intensely studied and is divided into five phases of development.

Recuay potters were the first to depict 'the common man'. Recuay ware is distinguished by its white paste, and by human and animal (most frequently feline) imagery, in white, black and red.

Nazca and early Tiwanku ceramics are highly polychrome styles. Nazca wares spread throughout the Nazca, Ica, Chincha, Pisco and Acari valleys. Modelling is infrequent (almost always of humans), while painting predominated, in up to 15 colours or shades of white, black, brown, red, yellow, purple and blue, as well as violet, orange, pink and grey. Complex scenes of intertwined

Below: A south-west coastal Peru Paracas drinking cup with typical geometric decoration reminiscent of textile patterns.

geometric patterns, deities, humans and animals cover whole pot surfaces, continuing the Paracas tradition.

Later Nazca potters changed from pre-firing painting to post-firing negative painting, using slips and wax to keep areas unpainted, paint resins delimited by incised lines to create a lacquer-like finish, and high polishing. Through several phases it evolved from more naturalistic to more abstract forms of decoration and imagery.

MIDDLE HORIZON MASS PRODUCTION

Growing political unity under the Tiwanaku and Wari empires spread their ceramics far and wide. Production was simplified and mass production in state-sponsored factories was introduced. Tiwanaku pottery is multicoloured on a distinctive orange base. Decoration is predominantly religious, depicting feline, serpentine and deity imagery (especially a figure holding staffs in outstretched hands), as on stone sculpture and textiles. Use of slips and colour range were similar to Nazca wares. A distinctive Tiwanakoid form is the tall *kero* drinking beaker; there were also huge, thick-walled, multicoloured storage urns set in pits.

In contrast, Wari pottery, also polychrome, is mostly secular. Geometric patterns and effigy vessels (both painted and moulded) predominate, and emphasis is on the world of humans. Towards the end of the Middle Horizon, decoration became more geometric and abstract, and quality declined.

CHIMÚ, CHANCAY AND INCA

The Chimú continued the Moche and Wari tradition of mass production using moulds, and decorating in several colours, but quality declined in favour of quantity. Plain polished black and red wares

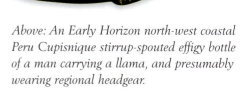

Above: An Early Horizon north-west coastal Peru Cupisnique stirrup-spouted effigy bottle of a man carrying a llama, and presumably wearing regional headgear.

were also made. Plates and ring-based bowls were introduced for the first time, and tripod bowls also became common; stirrup-spout bottles declined.

Central-coastal Chancay ware was another main style. Using crude, gritty clay, forms include oblong, narrow-necked bottles and jars with handles. Human faces were painted in grey-black on white slip backgrounds; there were also nude female effigies with outstretched arms.

Inca ceramics are characterized by painted decoration in black and white on red. Designs are geometric, especially fern motifs, triangles and rhomboids. Bird and animal imagery is stylized to the point of being abstract. Characteristic shapes are flat, round plates, *kero* cups and pointed-base, globular bottles with flared necks and handles.

INTERPRETING THE POTS

Two categories of ceramics co-existed in Andean civilization: utilitarian and special. The groups were not exclusive – the same forms were used for both – but wares for daily use were not necessarily made by specialists. Special wares, although functional, were meant for ceremonial and ritual uses, and some forms, such as animal-shaped incense burners, were clearly purpose made. Despite changing decorative styles and predominant techniques of manufacture in different areas, there were several common symbolic motifs and imagery that reflected pan-Andean religious beliefs.

CULTURAL RECORDS

Even highly decorated utilitarian wares, produced for social elites, served simultaneously, consciously or otherwise, as a record of culture by depicting mythological scenes and scenes of daily life as well as holding liquids and food.

Below: An Early Intermediate Period Pashash lidded jar with geometric, textile-like decoration and the image of a double-headed serpent, probably representing duality.

Right: Vivid subjects and delicate images decorate many Nazca pots, such as this bridge-spouted bottle depicting hummingbirds sipping nectar from a flower.

Spanish documents make almost no mention of pottery, so it is only through archaeology and comparison of the imagery on ceramics with our knowledge of Inca and earlier religion that we can surmise what the decoration meant.

The effort taken, especially by potters up to the Late Intermediate Period, to decorate pottery obviates its importance to convey messages to those making and using it. As well as being purely aesthetic, the ritual use of pottery shows that it was made for specific purposes. Making pieces especially for burial with the dead emphasizes the importance of the afterlife and the need to prepare for it.

Pottery models of houses and temples give us a rare insight of how reconstructions of the archaeological excavations of their foundations might look.

RELIGIOUS MEANINGS

In the Early Horizon, Chavín religious influence became widespread through symbolism, especially of feline, serpentine and cayman imagery, on portable artefacts – pottery, textiles and metalwork. The snarling feline with bared teeth and long canines, and serpent heads and bodies are thought to symbolize the power of these creatures and admiration of them. They were depicted through all the techniques – painted, incised in outline and moulded – showing their universal application across styles.

The snarling feline motif all but disappeared in the Early Intermediate Period, to reappear in Moche and later ceramics, again both as incised and painted imagery. The mouth is often wide open, and feline features are often combined with human features to represent transformation by shamans or priests. Bird and other animal transformation is also represented.

Imagery in different regions hints at predominant economic strengths, such as marine creatures on coastal wares. But the appearance of tropical animals (jaguars, caymans and tropical birds) on highland wares also shows the strength of highland–lowland contacts and the supernatural regard for those creatures by highland peoples.

Other deity imagery includes the Staff Deity, which characterizes Chavín, Tiwanaku and Chimú art, including on ceramics. Other local deities are also represented, such as the Oculate Being, which was so important in south coastal Paracas and Nazca culture.

THEMES

A ritual theme in Moche ceramics is the 'presentation scene', a simpler form of which also appears on Chancay pottery. In it, one figure, dressed in a shirt, short kilt and conical helmet, proffers a goblet to a seated or more prominent figure. There are also scenes showing cloth being offered.

A prominent theme in Paracas and Nazca pottery shows a deity or masked semi-human holding a severed head – trophy heads also being an important image in other media.

Below: Painted ceramic vessel with a snake-shaped handle from the Tiwanaku culture.

Above: A ceramic vessel from the Recuay culture (c.300–600AD) showing a snake with a feline head.

REMINDERS OF LIFE

The apparent exuberance of Nazca and Moche ceramics reveals the importance of the images and scenes as reminders to people of what was important. The portrayal of everyday narrative scenes, as well as more exotic events, from healing, to sex, to architectural models, and the care and time taken to mould and paint them, reveals the richness of life.

In Moche art, the ritual combat scene is often repeated, and Moche potters are the only ones known who definitely portrayed actual living people. One Moche man was portrayed 45 times, documenting much of his life. But whether depicting a living person or a type, Moche potters covered the range of human conditions from youth to old age and from health to sickness in effigy vessels showing backache, birth, healing and death.

The complex battle scenes on Nazca pottery contrast with ritual single-combat scenes on Moche pottery. Both, however, reveal an importance in conflict and in the ultimate outcome of sacrifice and death.

CONVENTIONS

Certain 'rules' of execution can also be detected in the uniformity and the stylization with Nazca and Moche pottery. Slip colours are only white or red. Background colours, on which detailed Nazca scenes were painted, are only painted in black, white or shades of red. Mythical beings on Paracas and Nazca pots are always shown frontal, and they are usually associated with severed heads.

Moche potters used conventions in the poses and actions of their animal, human and semi-human figures. The space between the feet indicated whether the figure was standing, walking, running or dancing. The angle of the torso and positions of the limbs showed speed, falling over or death. Despite such conventions, it is thought that the nuances of style in finishing and depicting facial features in the repetitious mould-made and painted forms sometimes reveals the hand of the same artist.

POWER AND CONTROL

The mass production of repetitious forms by the Wari, Tiwanaku, Chimú and Inca empires was a statement of power. It served to remind subjects of state control of production and provision of employment, alongside regulation of the economy.

SCENES AND PORTRAITS IN POTTERY

One of the most exuberant styles was the 'narrative' and 'portrait' pottery of the Moche. Like their revealing wall frescoes, tens of thousands of Moche pots depict scenes of everyday life: weavers, fishers, hunters, warriors, shamans, animals and plants. The scenes are painted in red lines on cream backgrounds (known as fine-line ware) on bowls, jars, cups and bottles. In addition, moulded effigy vessels were made in seemingly endless forms showing all manner of life scenes.

Moche mass production reveals state control of the industry and an imperial message that they were in control. As the Moche spread their empire by conquest, they stamped their style on other cultures through clay rather than textiles. Moche pottery has been found as far south as the Chincha Islands off the central coast of Peru, where Moche sailors in reed boats collected rich guano to fertilize agricultural fields back in the homeland.

Below: A red clay model of a house, probably Late Intermediate Period Chimú, shows us a domestic scene of seeming merry-making.

MOCHE VIRTUOSITY

There are lively and dexterous scenes in both media – fine-line and effigy. They are both aesthetically pleasing, even 'touching', and graphically revealing, for they show ritual as well as common life, individual portraiture as well as fantasy, and thus give us an astoundingly detailed picture of Moche culture, rich in the everyday and in the spiritual meaning of Moche beliefs. They depict both the ideal and the particular. On some they show, or are modelled as, individuals whose clothing and regalia announce their high rank and authority; others disclose their occupation or activity; others reveal a state of religious, drug-induced trance; and still others in everyday wear are occupied in ordinary tasks.

One animated scene painted around a globular vessel depicts a seal hunt. A line of presumably shallow shore waves underlines a violent scene of two hunters with clubs among a herd of seals, which flee in all directions from their pursuers. Shorebirds circle overhead and there is an island with spots, presumably meant

Above: Nazca religion featured a cult of trophy head collection. Here a bridge-spouted bottle has been painted as a trophy head, with stitched-up eyes and a pinned mouth.

to represent guano. The seals' arched bodies and outstretched, clawed limbs imply dynamic movement. Some are vertical, as if leaping into deeper waters and diving to avoid being clubbed. Two of them have been caught, their flippers flailing at right angles from their bodies and the hunters' clubs smacking against their heads. The seals are clearly frantic with fear as they attempt to elude the hunters. They have gaping mouths and dilated pupils within wide, white eyes.

Such dynamism is shown time after time. Battle scenes show warriors engaged in 'gladiatorial combat', in which the background, and the armour and weapons show both to be Moche, rather than captive warriors of other states. They fight in scrublands near the Moche cities. He who is defeated must undergo a gruesome ritual sacrifice, an act also depicted on pottery in exquisite detail with fully armoured warriors with helmets, shields and war clubs leading naked losers, their genitalia exposed as a sign of submission and with rope nooses around their necks.

SCENES OF DAILY LIFE

Effigy vessels show equally remarkable scenes. For example, a stirrup-spout bottle depicts a shaman or curer administering to a reclining, sick individual. The curer is a woman with a long shawl-like headpiece. She lays one hand on the body of the sick person, her other hand to her mouth. Perhaps she is chanting or attempting to suck the illness out. Next to her lies a severed head, perhaps to indicate that she will be executed if unsuccessful in curing her patient. There are fine-line drawings on pots showing curers' nude corpses being pecked by birds!

Other vessels show priests taking coca snuff. Another is the charming figure of a man bent over a flaring bowl, both hands stroking the water from his hair, which is curved over the bowl. Is he simply washing his hair, or engaged in some preparatory ritual before a religious ceremony? Another shows a hunter with a blow-dart tube shooting a bird in a tree.

Below: A Nazca bridge-spouted effigy bottle portraying a tattooed old, bearded man, who appears to be blind.

Right: One of hundreds of Moche red-ware portrait bottles. His distinct facial features, earrings and headpiece identify him as a living man whose face was copied in a mould.

Another stirrup-spout bottle is shaped as two warriors. The loser flees from his adversary, his head turning back and tilted up with the force of the blow as the war club of his opponent strikes his forehead. The winner's eyes and mouth reveal menace and grim determination; the loser's shows fear and drooping-lipped despair.

One pot shows a man tied with ropes to a tree. He is presumably a criminal. Above his tilted head a vulture stands on a branch pecking out his left eye.

Intimate scenes of sex are not eschewed, for effigy pots show images of embracing heterosexual and homosexual couples.

All manner of animals are sculpted as pots. Three such stirrup-spout bottles are an enchanting llama complete with panniers holding miniature bottles; a captivating reclining doe licking the nose of her fawn; and a humorous monkey, sitting with wide-open mouth and a *pepino* fruit clutched in his hands, just about to enjoy his meal.

PORTRAITURE

Finally, and perhaps most remarkably, there are the hundreds of portrait vessels. Many are unique: they depict perhaps an individual or at least a type – young and old people, musicians, healers; people laughing, smiling, frowning, contemplative, worried and frightened, ailing, wide-eyed and narrow-eyed, scheming, chubby-faced and lean, some moustachioed and bearded. They wear all manner of dress and individual hats and jewellery.

Christopher Donnan has recognized more than 750 distinct individuals. Of most there is only one example; but several have three or four portraits. One remarkable individual, with a distinct scar on his left upper lip, was a chosen gladiator who survived many bouts, for he was depicted at least 40 times, and has been dubbed 'Cut Lip'.

CHAPTER FIVE

FIBREWORK, COSTUME AND FEATHERWORK

The importance of cloth and fibre arts in Andean civilization cannot be underestimated. Fibrous plants were among the earliest domesticated plants. Mostly utilitarian at first, in time cloth became the most important exchange commodity other than food, and in Inca times served, in value, as a sort of 'coinage' of the realm.

Preceramic peoples worked plant fibres by simple twisting, twining and looping, making twine and bindings for spear, arrow and drill points, bolas stones and for slings. Sleeping mats, sandals and simple clothing were made with simple looping, as were nets, bags and carriers. These were the first steps towards the sophisticated weaving that became a hallmark of Andean civilization.

All women wove. In pre-Inca times textile production may not have been so exclusive to women, but in Inca society spinning and weaving were symbolic demonstrations of womanhood and they were done by all women, from the most common subject, through the noblewomen of the imperial household to the Sapa Inca's principal wife.

The importance of textiles to the Inca is epitomized in a statement attributed to Atahualpa, last Inca emperor, upon meeting Pizarro in Cajamarca: "I know what you have done along this road. You have taken the cloth from the temples, and I shall not leave until it has been returned to me." This, despite the Inca wealth in gold and silver!

Left: A late Early Intermediate Period Nazca or early Middle Horizon Wari poncho with stylized bird and animal imagery.

TWINING, SPINNING AND WEAVING

The variety and quantity of Andean textiles that have survived are phenomenal. Whereas ancient Mesoamerican textile studies are greatly reliant on pictures in ancient manuscripts (*códices*), Andean preservation has provided thousands of examples to study directly.

USEFUL *AND* SYMBOLIC

Late Archaic and Preceramic peoples twisted and twined wild plant fibres primarily for utilitarian objects. Twine and cordage provided binding for spear, arrow and drill points, and for bolas stones and slings. Looped cordage enabled them to make a variety of basic 'textiles' such as simple clothing, and various nets, bags

Below: A Moche red-line ceramic dish showing an old woman (left, with wrinkles) allegedly instructing a younger woman in the art of weaving, and talking, or possibly chanting or singing.

and carriers. Containers were fibre sacks, as well as animal skins, dried gourds and wooden vessels, before the discovery or invention of fired ceramics.

Utilitarian uses never ceased, however (footwear, mats, tools and bags required constant quantities of twine and cordage, and ordinary daywear required plain woven cloth), and remained important right through to Inca times. For example, quotas of cordage were required of male Inca subjects for the many bridges and army weapons needed. Cords dyed and knotted into *quipus* provided a means of keeping imperial accounts.

Soon, however, alongside developments in irrigation agriculture, monumental architecture and sophisticated religious beliefs, cloth became more symbolically utilitarian, as a medium for conveying religious concepts, for social and regional differentiation in clothing styles, and for preserving the dead.

Above: Llama wool spinning and weaving in the Andes was developed simultaneously with coastal cotton fibre use from the 1st millennium BC.

TEXTILE PRODUCTION

Plant fibres were simply shredded, dried and twisted into twine and cord, then knotted and looped (weft twisted around weft) into bags, baskets, sandals and other items. The earliest items are of hemp-like brome and agave plant fibres from Guitarrero Cave, dated *c*.8000BC. Cotton was one of the first Andean domesticated plants. It was grown in the coastal valleys of Peru and Ecuador from *c*.3000BC, although its wild ancestor must have been collected and tended earlier, before it was actively cropped.

By the 3rd millennium BC (Initial Period), cotton textiles were being made from Ecuador, through Peru to northern Chile. The llama and alpaca were domesticated in the Altiplano around the Titicaca Basin during the Preceramic Period. Evidence is lacking, but it is assumed that llama and alpaca wool spinning and weaving developed during this period and through the Initial Period, for there is ample evidence in the Early Horizon of wool used in Paracas embroidery on the south coast. Some wool use was found at Preceramic Aspero, but it was not until the Early Intermediate Period that wool was used extensively by central and north coastal peoples.

Above: A Chancay Late Intermediate Period wool and cotton tapestry cloth demonstrates the constant contact and interchange between coastal plains and mountains.

Nearly three-quarters of the early cotton textiles from Huaca Prieta are twined; the remainder are woven, or looped as netting. Twining does not involve a loom. The vertical warp threads are diverted slightly right and left and held by twisted horizontal weft threads – thus the weft turn around the warp rather than interweaving with it. The process is manual. Using different coloured threads enables the maker to produce patterns and pictures by trading the warp threads from the front to the back of the cloth, creating zigzag designs and images.

Loom weaving began in the Initial Period, from *c.*2000BC, with the invention of heddles – flat sticks to raise groups of threads in order to weave between them quickly – and the backstrap loom. Twining died out, but looping and sprang (interlinking sets of cloth elements) continued to be used for bags and hats.

Cotton was spun by beating the fibres out, rolling them into a cylinder and attaching it to a post, then drawing out the thread while twisting the cylinder. Wool was spun with the drop spindle.

LOOMS

All the techniques used by ancient Andeans for textile production were known by the end of the Early Horizon (*c.*200BC). In addition to knotting, looping and twining, these were: the plying of several strands (of wool) together;

Below: The continuous need for wool and cotton thread and yarn for weaving required daily drop spinning by women of all ranks in the Inca Empire and earlier (depicted in Poma de Ayala's Nueva Corónica, c.1615).

braiding; the use of discontinuous warp and weft to create imagery and patterns, also of supplementary warp and weft threads and complementary sets of warp or weft; warp wrapping (creating the design on the warp by wrapping it in coloured yarn before weaving); embroidery and tapestry; textile painting; tie-dying; and the use of double and triple cloth (interconnected layering).

Most ancient Andean weaving was done on backstrap looms, although other types were known, especially the vertical (suspended) loom. Warp threads were wound in a figure of eight around two posts. The warp ends are tied to wooden bars, one of which is fixed to a post or wall peg and the other to a backstrap around the weaver's waist. Warp tension is adjustable by leaning back or easing up.

Warp sheds are created, first, by the figure of eight of the preparation, then by lifting alternate warps on loops of thread called leaches, attached to a heddle stick. Weft threads are passed through the sheds, as they are lifted and lowered, with thread on a bobbin, then beat down against the earlier wefts. By lifting different sets of warps in sheds less than the entire width of the cloth, and/or by passing the weft through less than the full-width shed, patterns and images can be created within the warp and weft.

EARLY COTTON TEXTILES

Wild cotton relatives grow in northern Peruvian coastal valleys. Evidence of fibre use at Archaic Guitarrero Cave, and widespread production of cotton textiles from Ecuador to northern Chile at late Initial Period coastal sites, indicates millennia of wild cotton collection and tending before planting and extension of its cultivable range. Truly domesticated cotton (*Gossypium barbadense*) grows at 320–1,000m (1,050–3,280ft) above sea level.

COTTON DESIGNS

Lowland textiles are dominated by cotton, although llama wool, as it became more available through highland–lowland trade from the late Initial Period, was increasingly combined with cotton, especially at Paracas. Cotton takes dyes less easily than wool, so use of wool increased

Below: A Middle Horizon Wari woven poncho of wool and cotton fibre, with characteristic geometric patterns (some are possibly highly stylized faces), reveals trade for fibre between coastal cotton growers and Altiplano llama herders.

the colour range through the Early Horizon. Textile painting was also developed on the coast, perhaps for this reason.

Preceramic coastal fishing peoples relied heavily on cotton for knotted nets and line, found at most sites, including nets up to 30m (98ft) long.

Preceramic Huaca Prieta produced some of the earliest cotton fabrics, of which more than 9,000 fragments were found. Their designs show the earliest Andean concerns with visual messages, including multiple meaning and composite imagery. Complex patterns and imagery were created using twining with spaced wefts and exposed warps of different colours (red, yellow, blue, black dyed, and natural white and brown cotton), plus looping and knotting, in characteristic zigzag contours.

Human, bird, serpent, crab, fish and other animal imagery was used singly and in repetitive interlocking patterns. Multiple meanings are conveyed in double-headed birds and snakes, crabs that transform into snakes, and other creatures with multiple attributes. One famous piece portrays

Above: A painted, cotton Paracas, southern coastal Peruvian burial wrap depicts Staff Deity figures within diamond panels, revealing the influence of the Chavín Cult from farther north.

a raptor with spread wings, and a snake inside its stomach. Similar imagery is found on textiles from Asia and La Galgada.

CHAVÍN TEXTILES

Early Horizon Chavín textiles include more than 200 pieces from Karwa and other southern coastal sites, where they have survived. They include the earliest painted Andean textiles. It is assumed that highland Chavín sites used similar textiles. Northern coastal Cupisnique weavers also painted cotton textiles.

Karwa textiles were a medium for the spread of the Chavín Staff Deity. Female Staff Deity imagery was painted in brown and rose on plain woven cotton cloth. Sometimes several pieces were sewn together, for example a circle of jaguars

reminiscent of the circular sunken court jaguar sculptures at Chavín de Huántar. Cloth belts resemble that on the Lanzón Stela and many painted figures carry staffs or San Pedro cacti.

Karwa textiles always portray supernatural beings as female. Eyes substitute for breasts; fanged mouths for vaginas; and they carry plant staffs, often intertwined, or as animated cotton plants and bolls. Profiled attendants are either male or genderless. Like the Raimondi Stela at Chavín de Huántar, the female images present a second image when inverted. It is thought that she portrays an Earth goddess, and that the pieces are hangings, canopies and altar covers. Other fragments are clothing or mummy wraps. Braiding around textile edges is thought to be a symbol of continuity.

PARACAS TEXTILES

Contemporary Paracas weavers developed embroidery, using imported alpaca wool from the Altiplano on cotton backing cloths, sometimes also incorporating tropical bird feathers. They also invented discontinuous warp and weft techniques. By not passing the whole lengths of weft or warp threads across or down the loom, they could make highly complex woven imagery and patterns.

Hundreds of mummy bundles in the Paracas Cerro Colorado, Arena Blanca and Wari Kayan cemeteries include rich textile wraps. Bundles range widely from rough cotton mantles to elaborate multiple-bundle wraps of plain and highly decorated textiles, holding gold, feather, animal-skin and imported shell offerings. (Incorporating grave goods was a means of maintaining an individual's integrity and possession.) The largest bundles are up to 2m (6½ft) tall, and the largest cloths are 3.4 × 26m (11ft × 85ft)!

Paracas embroidery covers the whole of the ground cloth in vibrant colours, patterns and images. Motifs and imagery are usually applied at borders, neck-slits and in columns in the centres of mantles

or wraps. The textiles include the work of masters and apprentices – many cloths have a central panel of perfectly formed figures flanked by panels less well executed, attempting to copy the master's panel. Some cloths appear to be practice pieces; some are unfinished before burial. Calculations of the hours taken to make these complex pieces and multiple mummy wraps indicate that they occupied lifetimes, suggesting that preparation was specifically for burial.

LINEAR AND BLOCK COLOUR

The linear style comprises stitches sewn in and out of the ground cloth, always moving forwards and leaving visible lines of thread. In contrast, Block Colour style covers the thread by stitching forwards, then half backwards, then forwards again with slightly overlapping diagonal stitches. Linear textiles are more restrictive than

Above: A complex Initial Period Paracas embroidered burial shroud, made of fine alpaca wool, with dual central figures. The figure with the golden diadem is probably the Oculate Being and the other a shaman in a drug-induced trance, plus serpent and trophy head imagery.

Block Colour ones, being limited to straight lines of thin colour in red, green, gold or blue, while more expansive Block Colour textiles have blocks of solid colours and outlined, curved figures and patterns, and a colour palette of 19 colours and shades. Linear designs accommodate the shape of the long, flying Oculate Being. Motifs and imagery are not restricted to borders but often occur in cloth centres and as symmetrical arrangements.

Moche and Nazca textiles continued Early Horizon techniques and themes into the Early Intermediate Period.

WOOL FROM THE HIGHLANDS

Camelid llamas and alpacas were fully domesticated by *c.*2500BC. The process lasted several thousand years in the grasslands of south-central Peru around Lake Junin and the Altiplano around the Lake Titicaca Basin. Their domestication is evident from the steady decline in deer remains and the increase in camelid bones at late Archaic and Preceramic Period sites.

THE IMPORTANCE OF WOOL

Llamas were bred for three reasons: their meat, their carrying capacity and their wool. Llama wool, heavier and greasier than alpaca wool, was woven primarily for coarse cloth used for heavy-duty articles such as mats, sacks, saddlebags and cordage. Softer, longer alpaca wool was spun and woven for clothing and other fabric. Still finer, softer, wild vicuña wool was highly prized, especially by the Incas, who captured vicuñas for shearing in special hunts.

Alpacas and llamas were shorn between December and March and their wool spun simply by pulling and arranging the fibres to lie parallel, then winding the resulting 'roving' around the forearm or on a wooden distaff, and spinning it with a wooden drop spindle.

Below: Llamas herded for wool also served as pack animals in caravans, carrying goods between the highlands and lowlands.

Wool has two advantages over cotton: its staple is a longer fibre, which spins and adheres more readily, and it will take dyes more easily, thus increasing the range of colours and shades available for design. In Chimú weaving, cotton was almost always spun and used as single strands, whereas llama and alpaca wool threads were almost always plied: spun, then, two strands plied together. Spinning and plying were usually in the same direction.

WOOL EMBROIDERY AND DWW

Spun alpaca wool became prominent in Paracas embroidery, which provides some of the earliest combinations of cotton and wool (the wool embroidery being done on plain cotton cloth).

Paracas and Nazca weavers made huge quantities of wool and cotton cloth for everyday use and for burial clothing and wraps. With a wide colour palette, the hours required to produce large cloth wraps, both as wool embroidery on cotton backing and as discontinuous warp and weft (DWW) designs, shows that it was a major occupation.

Above: A Late Intermediate Period Chancay woollen tunic with 'pink' flamingos, native to the Peruvian coast. Such finely woven cloth was worn by individuals of high rank.

Religious imagery was especially important. The principal Paracas and Nazca creator, the Oculate Being, was portrayed in many forms. A wide-eyed being, he is associated with water and the sky. Usually shown horizontal, as if flying, he faces front with large, circular, staring eyes and long, streaming appendages, an attribute easily achieved both with line stitching and DWW. Such streamers often end in trophy heads or small woven figures. In some cases he wears a headband like the gold headbands found on buried mummies.

Other themes are birds, serpents and shamans with streaming hair, frequently as scores of small, twinned and repeated figures. In the Linear embroidery style, Oculate Beings or serpentine figures are often interlocking in a continuous border around the cloth edge and in strips across its width.

Left: A woollen Paracas burial shroud features a main central figure wearing a horned headpiece, probably the Oculate Being, but revealing Chavin Cult influence.

usually in repetitive, interlocking patterns. The work was mostly in cotton, with wool worked in as superstructal patterns. Humans or deities wear large headdresses or have rayed heads. Some tapestries feature repeated small human figures with crescent-shaped headgear, surrounded by raptors holding trophy heads. Central coastal Chancay weavers began to make 'gauze' cloth – open weaving in which the image is almost invisible in the net-like fabric unless held against a dark background.

The Incas honoured local weaving traditions, but introduced standardization in cloth production. In organized textile workshops at provincial capitals and principal towns, specialist weavers produced regular quotas of cloth, mostly of interlocking tapestry with geometric patterns.

Below: A Nazca–Wari woollen bag with stylized animal motifs and fur fringes. Woollen bags served for personal possessions and as panniers for llama caravans transporting produce between regions.

TAPESTRY

Early Intermediate Period and Middle Horizon coastal weavers developed tapestry. As a convenient use of small lengths of wool of various colours, tapestry designs became extremely colourful and complex.

On the south coast, tapestry replaced embroidery in importance, depicting the same imagery as before, especially geometric designs. Painting on cotton cloth also became more important. On the central and northern coasts, cotton and wool tapestry continued side by side through the Early Intermediate Period. Imagery favoured double- and multi-headed snakes, fish and supernatural composite beings – humanoid snakes, birds and fish. Interlocking, stepped-fret geometric designs were also popular.

TIWANAKU-WARI TAPESTRY

New styles in wool weaving reached the coast in the Middle Horizon, originating in the highlands among Tiwanaku and Wari weavers. Environmental conditions in the highlands, however, preclude most preservation of fabrics from these sites, from which only poor examples survive.

Tunics and hangings depict the imagery seen on Tiwanaku pottery and stone sculpture. The central, staff-bearing, ray-headed deity on the Gateway of the Sun is frequently portrayed, sometimes as a central figurehead surrounded or flanked by smaller staff-bearing figures. Winged figures known as 'angels' copy the 'attendant messenger' figures on the same monument. Mountain pumas and condors also came into more prominence as images.

LATE INTERMEDIATE AND LATE HORIZON CLOTH

Coastal weavers continued split-woven and DWW tapestry, combining cotton and wool. Feline, serpentine, avian and fish imagery became extremely complex as interlocking patterns of figures, similar to imagery on ceramics and mud wall sculpture; there were also dignitaries, shamans or deities with elaborate headdresses. The use of brocade – using extra wefts – was introduced as well.

Chimú and other north coastal weavers specialized in complicated geometric motifs in endless repetitions, plus jaguars and pumas, raptors and condors, fish and snakes,

GRASSES AND FIBRES

Grasses were an early and essential part of Andean economy. From Archaic times they continued to play an important role throughout Andean prehistory. Grass fibres were made into the earliest basketry and net bag containers before ceramics were discovered. Alongside gourds and wooden containers, baskets were used for the collection, storage and transport of wild plant foods.

EARLY CORDS

Few examples survive, but the regular twisting, looping and knotting techniques used by hunter-gatherers to make these articles suggest that there was a long period of development in techniques throughout the Lithic Period. None of the earliest examples shows patterning or decoration.

Below: One of the principal uses for totora reed by coastal peoples was for one-man fishing boats (today called caballitos *– 'little horses'), combining a local product to catch locally abundant fish. Depicted on Moche pottery, such boats are still used today.*

The earliest Andean fibrework comes from Guitarrero Cave in the north-central Andes. The dry cave deposits contained the earliest evidence of domesticated plants in South America, plants collected, then tended and deliberately planted, not for their food value but for 'industrial' and medicinal use, including hemp-like plants of the *Fuscraea*, *Tillandsia* and *Puya* species. These plants and fragments of the containers and other articles made from them predominate over plant foods and wood.

Containers, rough clothing, sandals and sleeping mats were made of simply twisted cordage. An open-mesh net bag from the lower cave deposits was made with simple knotting and looping. Other fragments of fabric show twining, with each weft strand manually twisted around the warp threads. A chert stone scraper from Guitarerro Cave, dated *c.*5500BC, has its butt wrapped in deer hide secured with twisted cord binding.

Use of plant fibres at Lithic Period sites is the beginning of the long association of fibre wrapping and important objects.

Above: A Late Intermediate Period Chancay ceramic effigy bottle, showing a man holding a small dog on a fibre rope, perched on his shoulder.

BODY SUPPORTS AND STUFFING

Another early use of 'fibres' was of sacred significance. The world's earliest mummies, dated *c.*5000BC, at Chinchorros in northern Chile were supported and bound with cane sticks and cords. After allowing the body to decompose, the bones were reassembled and supported by thin cane bundles tied with twine. Then the 'body' was remade by stuffing its cavities with fibre and feathers before sewing the dried skin over the body and applying a clay coating or mask. It is assumed that these practices were attempts to honour the spirit of the dead in the beginnings of ancestor cults.

CONTAINERS, BOATS AND BURIAL

Twined cord satchels, and reed and sedge baskets formed prominent parts of the assemblages at Huaca Prieta, La Galgada and other coastal villages. Some of the earliest ancient Andean textiles are also of

rough fibre, mostly from the cactus *Furcraea occidentalis* (an agave-like plant). Its sharp, pointed leaves can be crushed and shredded to produce fibres up 50cm (20in) long, which can then be twisted together to make cordage. The bast from a milkweed plant (*Asclepias*) was also used to make fibre. The leaves needed to be soaked for a long time before they could be beaten to release their fibres, then crudely 'spun' by rolling them between the palms or with the palm on the thigh.

Fishing peoples often combined (plied) fibre bast with cotton, especially when stronger cordage or netting was required. The strongest nets and basketry were made from grasses alone.

Cotton, wild and later domestic, was essential for Preceramic coastal fishing villagers for lines and nets. In their fishing and foreshore shellfish-collecting economy, however, they also needed basketry for

Below: Rope making was a labour tax in the Inca Empire. Every man was required to produce a specified quota of cordage for rope, especially to make and repair bridges.

collection and storage, and reeds for their fishing boats. They grew totora bulrush reeds specifically for boat making, as did peoples around the lakeshores of Titicaca and other mountain lakes. Reeds were also used for sails by Late Intermediate Period coastal fishers and traders. These watercraft traditions continue today.

Preceramic burials usually included at least a mat and plain cloth wrapping, if not more elaborate clothing. For example, the infant burial bundle at Huaca de los Sacrificios at Aspero was placed in a reed basket before being wrapped in textiles. Women were often buried with their weaving baskets, which were reed or sedge containers for spindles, threads and loom tools.

ARCHITECTURAL SUPPORT
Plant materials and rough fibre cordage played important parts in early housing and even in the earliest monumental architecture. For example, La Paloma coastal peoples lived in cane and reed huts with grass roofs. Thatch roofing was used by coastal and highland peoples right through to Inca times.

Above: Traditional use of totora reeds for roofing endures in these houses on a totora-reed 'floating island' near the shoreline on Lake Titicaca.

Plant chaff was an important element in mud-plaster architecture, providing a binding both for smooth plaster coverings on stone walls and in adobe brick walls.

The earliest platform mounds were built up with rubble before being finished off with impressive adobe brick or stone facings. Open-mesh satchels, called *shicra* in Inca times, made of split reeds and capable of holding as much as 36kg (80lb), were used to haul stone rubble. The baskets were not emptied, but were deposited *en masse* on the mound. The *shicras* found intact at late Preceramic El Paraíso each held 17.6–36kg (40–80lb).

In Inca times, men's role in the imperial textile taxation was to produce required quotas of cordage. Without strong cordage, Inca quarrying (rope for haulage), house building (cordage for roof binding) and bridge building (for suspension bridge cables) would not have existed.

CLOTHING STYLES

In ancient Andean society, cloth was wealth: it was exchanged between rulers, given as rewards for good service, and used to fulfil reciprocal obligations between members of kinship *ayllus*. It was important in the relationship between state and subject, and was presented at public ceremonies as items in the redistribution of wealth. Special clothing marked changes in life cycles, both as costume for initiation ceremonies and as a mark of age, social status and distinction. Specific people wore specific clothes for specific occasions. Cloth was offered to the gods in burnt offerings, used to dress and preserve mummies, and offered in burials. Finally, cloth provided a medium for representing the gods and religious imagery reflecting cosmological concepts.

INCA CLOTH

The Incas defined two grades of cloth: fine cloth, called *qompi*, was divided into two sub-grades, for tribute fabrics and 'best' cloth for royal and religious use; and *awasca* cloth – a plain, coarser fabric – was for ordinary use.

Below: This llama wool hat with geometric designs from the Atacama Desert shows Tiwanaku influence.

Above: Intricately woven textiles such as this Paracas poncho burial wrap with flying Oculate Beings were the preserve of the rich.

The Incas encouraged diversity among their subjects, not least in maintaining local textile traditions and clothing styles. Regional patterns and imagery, costumes and headdresses were badges of ethnic identity, for these were regarded as having been designated by Viracocha the Creator himself.

Ephraim G. Squier described the importance of clothing diversity in his 1877 book, *Peru: Incidents of Travel and Exploration in the Land of the Incas*: "If they were Yungas, they went muffled like gypsies; if Collas, they wore caps shaped like mortars, of wool; if Canas, they wore larger caps … The Cañari wore a kind of narrow wooden crown like the rim of a sieve; the Huancas, strands that fell below their chin, and their hair braided; the Canchis, broad black or red bands over their forehead."

STYLE

Andean clothing was mostly un-tailored. Tunics or shirts were made from two rectangular panels of cloth, woven at the maximum width of the loom, then sewn together along one edge, folded in half, and sewn down the sides, leaving openings for the head and arms. Capes or cloaks were made from two or more cloths stitched together.

Because clothing is often found in graves, it is sometimes difficult to determine what was daily wear, ritual costume or clothing specifically for burial. The mummy bundles of Paracas and Nazca vary in their richness and in the number of layers of cloth. Elaborate mummy bundles, presumably of rich, higher-status individuals, wore a loincloth, embroidered cloth belt, tunic or short poncho, shoulder mantle and turban.

Much Andean clothing is depicted on pottery and stone sculpture. For example, 13 late Preceramic figurines from Huaca de los Idolos at Aspero portray 11 women wearing thigh-length skirts, but no sandals. Some wear flat-topped hats and square-beaded red necklaces (two such beads were actually found). The capes worn by the Initial Period mud-sculptured figures at Moxeke are not dissimilar to those on the later

Below: Distinctive regional textile decoration and headgear is revealed on painted pottery, as on this Nazca jar.

Paracas mummies. And the elegant male figurines from Initial Period El Mirador wear full-length, sleeveless tunics, but also have bare feet.

Nazca effigy pots wear ponchos and tunics like those on mummies, with decorated neck and sleeve borders. A figurine vessel of a panpipe player wears a plain tunic with star-shaped neck decoration; other Nazca vessels depict a man's tunic and a woman's shawl-like mantle with circular designs; and a Nazca double-spout, stepped-fret bottle shows warriors wearing tunics with fringed borders and lampshade-shaped hats.

Another Nazca double-spout vessel portrays a stout fellow in a plain loincloth, brown and white chequered shirt and a matching, tightly wrapped turban around his head.

Below: This Middle Horizon Tiwanaku woollen unku *tunic shows a more unusual diagonal pattern of different coloured rows of flowers, requiring an extremely complex weaving technique.*

HEADGEAR

Moche ceramics are especially revealing, featuring an astonishing variety of geometric decorations on tight-fitting headdresses. Some are long strips of cloth wrapped twice around the head and tied at the back.

Others are bandanna-style cloths fitted over the head, with the front end wrapped around to the back and tied. Some Moche figures wear tight-fitting short-sleeved shirts.

Equally distinctive are Tiwanaku-Wari box-shaped wool hats. Made up of five tapestry woven panels sewn together to form sides and top, their vibrant colours, geometric patterns, and rows of winged beasts, birds and abstract human figures resemble the imagery on ceramics. Some sport little points or tassels at the top corners.

Tiwanaku-Wari hangings and clothing were made with interlocking DWW weaving rather than the slit-weaving tapestry of the earlier coastal traditions. Imagery and patterns are elongated and compressed. Faces are frequently split up into small rectangular elements.

Tiwanaku-style tunics were made so that the warp threads lie horizontally across the chest rather than vertically (as in earlier coastal tunics). They were made of two rectangular cloths sewn down the warp edges, leaving an unsewn mid-section for the head of the wearer. Some Tiwanaku tunics were made of a single

Above: This Middle Horizon Wari mummy bundle reveals the wealth of the buried person by the sheer number of wraps to create the bulky mummy, including an outer unku *tunic, woven wool and fibre scarf and 'hair'.*

cloth, the head slit being made by a long section of discontinuous warp from each side. Likewise, Tiwanaku and Wari effigy pots show figures wearing just such hats and bordered tunics.

Inca 'factory-produced' cloth was primarily of interlocking tapestry tunics, also with the warp running horizontally across the chest of the wearer and mostly decorated with geometric patterns. Vicuña wool, and cloth embellished with gold, silver or feathers, was restricted to imperial and noble use.

RITUAL COSTUME

Much of the cloth created in the Early Horizon was for ritual purposes. The complex imagery and geometric patterns on rectangular lengths of cloth bore religious significance, reflecting Andean cosmological concepts. They were hangings, canopies and altar covers for the temples, and burial wraps.

PRIESTLY GARB

The figurines from the highland Initial Period site of El Mirador were found in an unusual ovoid building separated from, but close to, the main temple site of Pacopampa. The sculptures were especially finely made and other finds included Pacific shells, foreign ceramics and exotic figurines of felines, dogs, bears and chinchilla-like rodents. The temple included an elaborate drainage system, anticipating that at Chavín de Huántar. This evidence and context suggest association with the temple. The figures are thought to represent priests and the ovoid building a priestly residence. If this is correct, then their long tunics are presumably ritual dress, for their length would make them impractical for daily work. Similarly, the mud sculptures at Moxeke, in niches atop the main public platform, were clearly

religious figures. Two cloaked torsos are either priests or gods, whose missing heads may represent ritual beheadings. Although the capes are 'typically' Andean, one figure also wears a twisted cord sash and holds double-headed snakes, which might be part of the costume. Both wear short, pleated skirts.

These Initial Period finds suggest both that some clothing was special to the priestly function, while other garb, although essentially the same as daily wear, was more elaborate in its decoration and of finer quality. An effigy bottle from a looted tomb in the Jequetepeque Valley is exemplary. The small spouted bottle (26.8cm/10½in) portrays an elegantly attired man playing an ocarina. His tunic, like those made throughout Andean history, drapes over his body, but is especially richly decorated with stylized feline and avian figures, whose details are picked out in many colours.

SNAKE MEN

The wall sculptures in Chavín de Huántar's circular sunken court also depict priests in ritual costumes. They are composite creatures, representing gods, shamanistic transformation or priests

Above: A Chimú wooden figure with a mud mask, carrying a kero *cup. The mask, earrings and headpiece are probably ritual costume.*

acting out these roles. They wear collared, long-sleeve shirts, trousers (or perhaps just anklets?), elaborate, braided-snake headdresses and snake belts. They have strange, stepped-fret 'wings' on their backs, decorated with feline mouths. Their own mouths have huge canines and their feet and hands are talons. The whole scene is one of ritual procession and transformation, and the elaborate costumes of the priests can only have been made especially for such occasions.

The richly adorned mummy bundles of Paracas and Nazca are also difficult to interpret. The care and time involved in making the textiles, and the labour of preparing the burials, can be attributed only to ritual beliefs. Despite variation in the quality and quantity of textiles,

Left: The Inti Raymi winter solstice, revived in 20th-century Peru, brings out latter-day Incas in 'ancient' ritual costume.

these burials reveal social hierarchy, although it is uncertain whether the clothing was specifically for burial or also represents daily wear, according to rank. The records of elaborate, rich clothing worn by certain classes in later periods by Chimú and Inca nobility, however, suggests that the standard loincloth, tunic, mantle and turban were 'normal' wear, although there were perhaps pieces specially made for burial. Perhaps Paracas and Nazca priests enacted ritual myth dressed in the mantles so richly decorated with mythical imagery.

PRIESTS AND PRIESTESSES AS GODS

There is no doubt that the elaborate costumes worn by the priests and priestesses depicted in Moche murals and on pottery are ritual costume. The Sacrifice and Presentation ceremonies show them dressed in colourful tunics with decorated neck borders, belts, a pleated skirt on the priestess, and various extraordinary headdresses with tassels, crescent-knife shapes or bandanna styles.

There is little doubt, too, that the extremely rich burials at Sipán and San José de Moro represent individuals whose tasks were to impersonate these deities in the ritual. Their burial costumes are exactly those of the murals, showing the Warrior Priest, Owl Priest, and Priestess in feathered tunic. In addition to his gold and other jewellery, and gilded copper adorned capes, the Warrior Priest even wore ceremonial copper sandals.

Similarly, the gear worn by Moche warriors on pottery and murals, although undoubtedly the same as that used in battle, also represents ritual weapons and armour. It was a sort of gladiatorial combat, performed for religious purposes, the ultimate outcome of which was the sacrifice of the loser.

Equally revealing is the burial at Dos Cabezas of a tall Moche priest wearing a bat-motif hat. His tomb also included 18 other headdresses, assumed to be for the performance of his many ritual roles.

GOLDEN CAPES

Gold ornament was often applied to mantles, and it seems reasonable to assume that such clothing was not for everyday wear, with the exception of kings and emperors. Chimú weavers specialized in ritual garments incorporating

Left: An Early Horizon Chavín effigy pot portrays a shaman or priest with facial scarification, wearing a jaguar headdress and playing a flute, probably using ritual music to induce hallucinations.

Above: From the earliest times Andean ritual costume required materials and dye colours from far-flung regions. This Nazca headdress from southern Peru has tropical bird feathers, traded in from the rainforest.

rich patterns of coloured tropical feathers, gold and silver spangles, beads and tasselled edges.

Inca dress was of standard type for all, the difference being in the richness of the wool, the elaboration of decoration and colour, and the embellishment with gold, silver and feathers.

New clothing was made for boys and girls for their initiation rites. The rather elaborate costumes donned today in re-enactments of Inca rituals bear resemblance to ancient costume, but inevitably have been elaborated in combinations of colonial influence and modern imagination. Nevertheless, such re-enactments represent a statement of independence and resistance.

FEATHERS AND FEATHERWORK

Coastal and tropical rainforest bird feathers were important in Andean cultures from the Initial Period. Exotic tropical feathers were traded right across the Andes from the eastern lowlands and rainforests by coastal cultures.

Making feather costumes demanded great labour and conferred considerable importance to the wearer, advertising one's high status in society.

FEATHER OFFERINGS

In early periods, feathers were included in burials and caches as offerings. Ritual offerings on platform summits at late Preceramic Aspero included a buried offering of red and yellow feather arrangements. Loose green, pink, blue and yellow feathers and down were found beneath a floor at El Paraíso; a carved stick at Río Seco was covered with white feathers; and there were red and orange macaw feathers in burials at La Galgada.

Below: This Late Intermediate Period Chancay ceremonial headdress shows a characteristic chequered pattern and brilliant yellow tropical parrot feather decoration.

Below: Remarkable preservation in the Paracas Desert necropolis in southern Peru has left unspoiled a feather and rope-fibre fan and woven cotton bag decorated with tropical parrot feathers for holding personal burial items.

Among Initial Period burials at Ancón, one special individual was buried with a cebus monkey – covered with mica flakes and placed on his knees – and had strings of coloured feathers, iron pyrites and beads on his forehead. His head rested on a wooden bowl filled with coloured tropical feathers.

FEATHERED TEXTILES

Tropical feathers were also imported by Paracas and Nazca weavers. Feather decorations were inserted among embroidered patterns, and braided strips of cloth held long feathers to create a sort of tall bonnet. Feathers were also cached with gold, animal skins and exotic shells in burials.

By the Early Intermediate Period, elaborate ritual clothing included entire mantles of feathers. An unusual Nazca tunic is made of a cotton back-cloth covered in bright yellow tropical feathers, highlighting a turquoise 'running' monkey with yellow eyes, also of feathers. The monkey constitutes another connection between coastal peoples and rainforest tribes.

The Priestess in Mural E at Moche Pañamarca wears a distinctive feathered mantle in the Presentation Ceremony.

Middle Horizon cultures extended the use of feather garments as status items. A Wari mantle comprises intricately combined cream, orange, black and blue feathers to make two orange eight-pointed stars with faces, above an orange double-headed snake. The three elements are thought to represent duality and the four directions.

As well as actual feathers, Pukará, Tiwanaku, Wari and Lambayeque-Sicán Middle Horizon art features heads with rayed feathers. The most superb example is perhaps the gold mask from Huaca Loro Tomb 1 at Batán Grande: its human visage wears a tall headdress with a central vampire bat face and 90 delicate golden feathers.

CHIMÚ FEATHERWORK

Late Intermediate Period Chimú weavers were especially adept at incorporating feathers into costumes. On plain-weave

white cotton back-cloths, they sewed rows of tiny, bright red, pink, orange, yellow, green and blue tropical bird feathers, creating garments as brilliant and shimmering as those covered in thousands of tiny gold squares.

Feathers were attached by bending their quill ends over a thread of the back-cloth and fixing it with a second thread, which was knotted around the bend of each quill. Each feather-holding thread was stitched down to the fabric so that the feathers overlapped, hiding the cloth.

Bird feathers included: tinamou, cormorant, great and snowy egret, Chilean flamingo, Muscovy duck, Salvin's curassow, macaws (blue-and-yellow, Scarlet, red and green), parakeet, trogon, purple honeycreeper, and various Amazonian parrots and tanagers.

One Chimú poncho bears images of light blue pelicans made up of feathers, with red feather eye circles and beaks. Two large pelicans are borne on litters of red and green feathers, carried by smaller, blue-feather pelicans along a blue-feather road. An exemplary Chimú piece, a ceremonial headdress, combines white, yellow, black, grey, turquoise and pink feathers from flamingos, macaws, razor-billed curassows and parrots. Its main body includes two human figures wearing axe-crescent hats, below a flared crown of long white macaw feathers and stepped-fret decoration in pink, yellow and black. Even the eyes, mouths, fingers and toes are intricately rendered in different coloured feathers.

The expense of importing enough tropical bird feathers to cover entire tunics meant that only Chimú kings and nobles wore such clothing. They were ostentatious declarations of their power and wealth. The making of such garments required thousands of retained artists, supported by commoners through taxation.

INCA FEATHERWORK

Likewise, only Inca emperors and nobility wore feathered cloaks, and Atahualpa commissioned a mantle made from bat skins. The Chachapoyas of the north-eastern Andes, in Inca Chinchaysuyu, were specialist traders with Amazonian tribes for their tropical products, including feathers, to the Incas and the Chimú before them.

It is significant in this context that the roster of court officials in the legendary Naymlap's entourage includes one

Left: Detail from a Late Intermediate Period tunic of brilliant tropical macaw feathers from the Amazon, probably depicting a shaman in ritual trance.

Above: A Chimú ritual featherwork poncho, depicting a Staff Deity-like figure and different coastal birds and fish, reflecting the Chimú reliance on the sea.

Llapchillulli, 'Purveyor of Feathercloth Garments'. Clearly, valuable trade links for tropical feathers between the northern Peruvian coast and the eastern Andes and Amazonia were perpetuated for hundreds of years by Lambayeque-Sicán lords and their Chimú successors.

Inca featherwork was as important as, or even more valuable than, metalwork and cloth, because of its relative rarity. As well as being sewn on back-cloth for human garments, featherwork features in headdresses of great complexity, and also on miniature figurines. Some Inca ceremonial headdresses feature great crescents of long-tail raptor and condor feathers, as well as tropical bird feathers.

In addition to feather mantles and cloaks, Inca emperors, borne on litters, were shaded with macaw-feather parasols.

DRESSED FIGURINES

Andean peoples frequently used figurines as ritual offerings and in burials. Clay, metal and cloth figurines were 'dressed', mirroring their makers' clothing styles.

PAINTED AND ACTUAL CLOTHING

While some early figurines are naked, others wear clothing similar to cotton and woollen cloth found in excavations. There are, for example, late Preceramic figurines from Huaca de los Idolos of women wearing thigh-length skirts, flat-topped hats and square-beaded red necklaces; a rotund

Below: A Middle Horizon dated Chancay figurine of dyed cotton forming a face and body, plus garment wraps around cane and straw body and limbs.

Paracas burial figurine with a curious headband of circles and tube ornament, and incised-line and cream-painted clothing and 'shells' collar; tall Pacopampa figurines in long, sleeveless tunics; and numerous Nazca and Moche effigy vessels of people 'dressed' in typical garments.

At Initial Period Mina Perdida (2nd millennium BC), however, a fibre human effigy figure is made of a jointed, thread-wrapped gourd dressed in a cotton mantle. It was found face down on a platform terrace, and possibly represents a shaman in transformation, for it has condor markings on its face.

WOVEN FIGURE FRINGES

Many Paracas and Nazca cotton textiles feature fringes comprising rows of severed heads. Several, however, have rows of small woven human figures, *c.*30mm (1¼ in) tall. One such Nazca burial wrap shows a line of musicians, standing with arms in the air, or across their bodies, their hands holding tiny woven rattles or bells. Each wears a tunic with a decorated band at the hips.

MINUSCULE GOLD AND STONE CLOTHES

One of three earspools in Tomb I of the Moche Lord of Sipán depicts a tiny figure of Lord Sipán himself of astonishingly intricate workmanship. The tiny figure is dressed in a tunic made of polished turquoise chips, a gold mask (complete with miniature, movable, gold crescent-shaped nosepiece), a necklace of minuscule golden owl heads, minute gold belt bells, two minute circular gold and turquoise earspools, and a headdress of turquoise chips and gold *tumi*-knife crescent and stepped, golden 'horns'. He holds a round gold shield and a removable golden war club.

This figure is flanked by two even smaller warriors made of turquoise chips, each wearing a turquoise-chip tunic, necklace and multi-layered helmet with gold

Above: Two woollen textile figurines used as Late Intermediate Period Chancay funerary offerings, a female (left with longer tunic) and male (right), representing duality.

tumi-knife crescent. They also have gold and turquoise earspools and carry circular gold and turquoise shields.

At Wari Pikillacta, 40 tiny figurines, each about 25mm (1in) high, were made of tiny precious stones, and are 'dressed' in tunics, mantles and hats of gold foil, and belts of precious stone chips and shell.

THE WEAVING LESSON

An astonishing Late Intermediate Period cotton cloth 'sculpture', Chancay or Chimú, depicts a mother teaching her daughter to weave. The two tiny figures sit on a woven, stuffed 'pillow' with stripy white, black, red, orange and yellow decorations. The mother works a miniature backstrap loom fixed to a wooden 'post' stuck into the pillow. The loom is complete with warp and weft threads, wooden warp beam and shed sticks. She holds a heddle rod poised to insert into the miniature shed. She is inclined towards her daughter as if explaining her work, and a head cloth of loose-weave, orange and yellow chequered pattern that resembles Chancay open-work weaving covers her long, dark brown hair.

Below: An Inca gold figurine, richly dressed in woollen clothing held with a miniature gold tupu *pin. Such figures represented* mamaconas *or* acllas, *the chosen women of the imperial court, and were sometimes deposited in child sacrifice burials.*

Her daughter sits beside the loom, her own long hair arranged in a minute topknot, spilling from a close-fitting hat with stripes and minute animal-heads decoration.

Both mother and daughter wear robes with stripy patterns and fringed bottoms. Details of their eyes, including pupils, noses and mouths are rendered in minute stitches.

Not only is this piece astonishing for its detail, but it is also one of the few actual images showing us ancient Andean weaving.

CLOTH 'DOLLS' AND DRESSED METAL

Many Late Intermediate Period Chancay burials contain offerings of cloth 'dolls'. Reminiscent of earlier Nazca fringe figures, they are of wrapped yarn and embroidered fabrics. Facial features and hair, stick-like arms and fingers, and decorated clothing are all of woven and stitched threads.

Inca gold and silver figurines of nude men and women have been looted from and found in undisturbed sacrificial child burials, often on remote mountaintops. Some are dressed, and miniature clothing has been found separately elsewhere, indicating that all such figurines were dressed. Their clothing was possibly removed for some sacred moment in the sacrifice ritual or burial ceremony.

The silver Cerro del Plomo figurine from Chile wears a brown and white mantle over a similar tunic. Both have strips and edges of red and yellow decoration. The mantle is tied

Above: A Late Intermediate Period Chancay reed figurine with cotton textile features, hair and clothing – probably a funerary offering.

with a tiny, decorated cord with rectangular shell toggles, and held with a miniature silver *tupu* pin. A magnificent, brilliant, red feather semicircular headdress crowns the head.

Two gold figurines from a burial of three sacrificed children on Mount Llullaillaco, Argentina, were equally magnificently dressed. Both wear white wool mantles, with red, yellow and black, and red and black borders. One is female, with gold and silver *tupus* pinning her mantle. Her long, tightly bound hair is moulded in gold, and a headdress of red and orange feathers frames her face.

The male figure has large, looped earpieces and a close-fitting cap, both moulded in gold. His mostly white mantel covers a red, yellow and black tunic, and he wears a grey turban with a sheet-gold ornament fixed to the front with a red and gold-headed pin, and an array of yellow feathers at the back.

CHAPTER SIX

METAL, WOOD, STONE, SHELL AND BONE

Apart from ceramics and stone sculpture, few ancient Andean items are of a single material. Most metal artefacts are alloys of gold and silver, gold and copper or silver and copper. Many stone, wood and metal objects are embellished with stone and shell inlay.

With these materials and media, Andean craftsmen created exquisite objects as well as utilitarian tools. Even some of the most common objects were highly carved, shaped or decorated. Most techniques were known from the earliest times. Shells and exotic stones were made into beads in the Preceramic Period if not earlier, and the first gold foil dates from *c.*1500BC.

Exotic materials were sought throughout the Andean Area and beyond, including turquoise, lapis lazuli and spondylus, or thorny oyster, shell. Working with gold and silver was highly controlled.

These materials advertised an individual's social status, and yet their value was primarily in the objects they were used to create and in the religious symbolism they represented. Ancient Andeans had no defined monetary values or currency. Only the copper *naipes* found in bundles in Sicán-Lambayeque tombs at Batán Grande (but rare elsewhere) possibly had an agreed exchange value. Spanish chronicles report that "6,000 seafaring Chincha merchants" used copper as a medium of exchange with Ecuadorian peoples.

Left: A Lambayeque sheet gold burial mask with Sicán 'comma-shaped' copper inlay eyes and nose beads.

MINING AND METAL TECHNOLOGY

We know little about Inca or pre-Inca mining. The Spaniards, primarily interested in gold and silver, quickly took over these areas and imposed their own techniques in the first century after the conquest.

Abundant sources of gold, silver and copper in Peru and Bolivia are found pure (gold and copper) and in ores (silver and copper). Most prehistoric Andean gold was retrieved from streams by washing the gravel in wooden trays. Sometimes streams were diverted to expose gold-bearing gravels. Lesser amounts were excavated from one-man trenches.

Mine shafts for silver and copper ores were 1m (1 yard) or so to perhaps 70m (230ft) long. Vertical shafts were only as deep as the dirt could be thrown up to the surface, then another hole was started near by. Wooden, bronze and antler tools were used to dig, and stone and deer antler hammers and picks were used to break up veins of ore, and to crush it. Excavated material was brought out in hide sacks and fibre baskets.

Spanish chroniclers record that Inca mines were worked only in the summer, from noon to sunset. Mining, like so many other tasks, was carried out as part of the Inca *mit'a* labour tax.

Crushed silver and copper ores were heated in clay crucibles to melt the metal and drain it from the ore. Relatively pure veins of copper yielded pieces that could be worked cold, as copper is relatively soft.

Above: Moche gold and turquoise necklace. Moche goldsmiths often combined gold beads with semi-precious imported stones.

Gold-bearing streams and ore deposits were considered sacred places. Ceremonies were held at them to honour their holy spirits and solicit ease of extraction. Gold and silver collection and mining were restricted under state control in the Inca Empire (and, as they were regarded as precious, probably under elite control in pre-Inca cultures as well). Copper extraction and use was widespread and less regulated.

METAL TECHNOLOGY

Andean metalsmiths were superbly skilled, and undertook extremely delicate work as well as large-scale pieces. They were specialized craftsmen, employed by the state or maintained as retainers of the elite to produce tools and exquisite items for elite consumption.

Left: Small figurines, such as this sheet-gold, sculpted llama, were made in abundance by the Incas, and often placed in the tombs of sacrificed children.

Objects were produced in small compounds, partly residential, partly workshop, where the metals were heated, hammered, bonded and formed into all manner of utilitarian and sumptuary objects.

Techniques included hammering into sheets to make the metal pliable, annealing, repoussé, incised and cut-out designs, joining and soldering, mould and lost-wax casting, gilding, burnishing and over-painting.

All of these methods were known in the Andean Area, although central Andean, Ecuadorian and southern Colombian metalsmiths preferred working with sheet metals and metal strands to create sculpture and jewellery, using sheet metal rolled, hammered and formed into objects and jewellery. Metalsmiths in northern Colombia and Central America favoured casting (including lost-wax casting, in which the figure is made of wax, then covered with clay, leaving a channel for molten metal to be poured in, which melts and drains away the wax; once the clay covering is broken, the object remains).

Utilitarian objects were made of copper and bronze, including knives, war club heads, agricultural hoes and digging implements, tweezers and beads. Gold and silver were used to make exquisite elite objects, including all sorts of jewellery, masks and figurines.

HAMMERING

Before being hammered, ingots of workable size were made from smaller pieces melted together. Hammering was done with hard, fine-grained stones (usually of magnetite, haematite or fine-grained basalt), formed into flat, round or cylindrical anvils and unshafted hammerstones, held in the hand. As hammering proceeded, the flattened sheet was annealed (reheated until it glowed red, then quenched with water) to prevent it from becoming brittle and cracking.

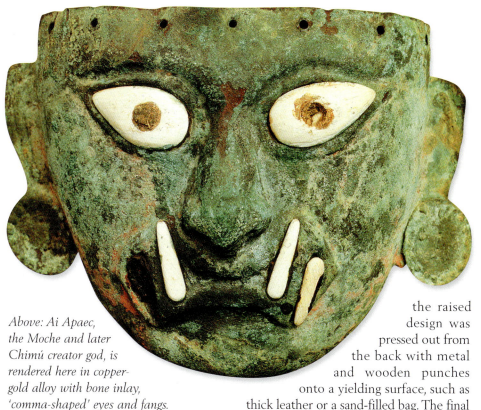

Above: Ai Apaec, the Moche and later Chimú creator god, is rendered here in copper-gold alloy with bone inlay, 'comma-shaped' eyes and fangs.

REPOUSSÉ AND INCISION

The process of repoussé – the creation of relief designs from behind – began with cutting out the shape with a thin-bladed chisel. The pattern was scribed onto the metal, sometimes using templates, then

Below: Using the lost-wax technique, the Muisca people made exquisite gold necklaces of identical tiny figurine 'beads'.

the raised design was pressed out from the back with metal and wooden punches onto a yielding surface, such as thick leather or a sand-filled bag. The final design was refined and sharpened from the front with fine tools.

Incised designs were also scored into metal figures, and areas of metal were sometimes cut out.

JOINING AND BONDING

Multi-piece objects, sometimes of different metals, were combined by several techniques. Edges were overlapped and hammer-welded, with annealing, sometimes including the clinching of the edges by folding them over on each other. Soldering and brazing were accomplished with melted bits of metal alloy. Moche spot-welding was second to none, with some pieces including hundreds of individual spot-solderings. Granulation, or diffusion bonding, was used for very fine work, such as tiny beads or fine wire. Copper compound and organic glue were applied at the joins of gold or silver parts, then heated to burn away the glue and form a copper-alloy brazed bonding.

Mechanical joins were formed in a variety of ways, including stapling, lacing with a metal strip, pinning and clinching.

Right: Inca metalsmiths made numerous solid silver (as here, with copper hairpiece) and gold male and female figurines.

MOULDING

Cast moulding was rare, as few pieces were solid. Chisels and axes were made in simple, open moulds of stone or clay, into which molten metal was poured.

FINISHING

Objects were highly polished, burnished with dried animal dung, wood, metal, leather and cloth. Sometimes the actual metal was over-painted. Many objects were gilded, using extremely thin gold foil.

PRECIOUS METALS AND EARLY METALWORK

All Andean metal that glittered was not gold, for Andeans were more interested in the essence of appearance. Most 'gold' objects were in fact alloys with a gilded surface. Alloys included tin and copper bronze, gold and silver, silver and copper or gold and copper (tumbaga). Different metals were also combined individually in pieces of work, as well as inlaid with stone, lapis lazuli from Chile and shell. Masks were often painted over, so hiding the metal!

VALUE AND SYMBOLISM

The production and exchange of sumptuary goods of all kinds was controlled by the elite in cities. Rather than a market economy, however, precious metal artefacts were used as items of prestige and as gifts and hospitality. Their value was in the political alliances they helped to seal and in the religious continuity and enforcement they secured. Most exchange was in the context of religious or political ceremony.

Below: The Chimú, successors of the Moche-Sipán and Lambayeque-Sicán north-west coast goldworking tradition, shod their buried kings with exquisitely fine leather sandals with sheet-gold clasp ornaments with turquoise inlays.

Gold and silver objects were widely traded, yet neither had a market value. What was important was the symbolism of the objects. Apart from tools, metalwork was devoted to elite objects meant to be used and worn by upper classes and as funerary offerings. Thus, commoners ate from pottery plates while Inca nobles used identical plates but made from gold or silver. Decoration always involved religious symbolism, either as images of the gods, sacrifice and sacred animals, or the symbolic representation of life (for example in exquisitely modelled animals, birds and agricultural plants). Cuzco even had a zoo–garden of gold and silver replicas.

The ultimate symbolism is expressed in the Inca concept of gold as 'the sweat of the Sun' and silver as 'the tears of the Moon'.

Above: Moche paired gold half-discs were embossed with solar flares or wave motifs – and may have been used as earrings or clothing ornaments.

EARLY METALWORK

The earliest known New World metalwork is gold. It comes from Waywaka, in the Andahuaylas Valley of the central Peruvian highlands. Here, a stone bowl contained a metalworker's tools, and a burial contained pieces of thin, beaten gold foil (nine pieces in the hand, with lapis lazuli beads, and one in the mouth), dated *c.*1500BC. The tools comprised a cylindrical, flared-top stone anvil and three stone hammers for beating the gold into foil.

Roughly contemporary, at Mina Perdida, on the central Peruvian coast, small pieces of hammered gold and copper foil

Right: La Tolita goldsmiths, in the far northern corner of Inca Chinchaysuyu quarter, were part of a northern tradition of smithing producing fine sheet-metal ritual objects, such as this Sun God mask with repoussé face and cut sheet-gold rays.

were found on its platform, dated *c*.1450–1150BC. Some pieces are gilded copper, and they appear to have been thrown from the ceremonial summit.

Slightly later, villagers of the Wankarani culture near Lake Poopó (south of Lake Titicaca) developed copper technology, as shown by pieces of smelted slag dated *c*.1200–800BC.

These mid- to late Initial Period finds are scant evidence of the prolific metallurgical technology subsequently practised in later periods throughout Andean civilization. Nevertheless, they demonstrate the early beginning of combining metals, 'essence' in representation through gilding, and the association of metal offerings both with burials and with religious ceremony.

EARLY HORIZON METALWORK

Metallurgy techniques in the Early Horizon period appear fully developed in comparison to the earliest finds, revealing that much intervening development must have taken place. Forged and annealed gold and silver figurines with Chavín motifs have been found at Chavín de Huántar and other Chavín sites. Soldering and repoussé were employed, as were alloys of gold, silver and copper.

Chavín–Chongoyape goldsmiths used sheet metal to make objects to inter or store in caches. Gold sheets were decorated in repoussé and rolled into tall cylinders, thought to be crowns, face masks, pectorals and smaller pieces for application to clothing. Their imagery is typically Chavín and Cupisnique: the Staff Being and feline faces. Characteristic Chavín obscurity or illegibility is achieved in complex, busy designs bordering on the abstract. Whole images are obscured in the curvatures, and sometimes the work is so complex that symbols are revealed only in the play of light and shadow.

Gold, 'wholly other' and immutable, incorporates a sacred message, and is the reflection of the sun. Gold on the outside, as gilding or on clothing, reflected the inner quality of the elite wearer.

A gold alloy pectoral disc from Chavín de Huántar depicts a central feline fanged face, while around the edge an interlaced

Left: A Chavín gold jaguar figurine with embossed pelt markings.

braid represents continuity and unity of the cult. A cylindrical crown from Chongoyape depicts in repoussé the full figure of the Staff Deity, with highly stylized staffs, snake-like swirls from its head and a flared-nostril feline face on the torso. Although it resembles the Staff Deity image on the Raimondi Stela at Chavín de Huántar, both pieces reflect the range of interpretation allowed within Chavín imagery as the cult spread north and south from the cult site.

PARACAS AND NAZCA METALWORK

Spanning the Early Horizon and Early Intermediate Period, Paracas, Nazca and Moche metalwork preserved many Chavín elements but also developed their own unique styles.

Gold objects placed in Paracas and Nazca graves of distinguished individuals reveal the growing differentiation in social hierarchy. Thin sheets of nearly pure gold were cut into elaborate silhouettes and decorated with sparse repoussé details, but highly polished to achieve maximum glitter. Mummy bundles include noserings, mouth and whole face masks, forehead ornaments, headdress plumes with sea animals, clothing discs and gold staffs.

MOCHE LORDS OF SIPÁN

The true glory of ancient Andean gold, silver and copper artistry comes to life in the rich tombs of the north-west Peruvian coast. Moche artisans were capable of the tiniest attention to detail, such as the kneecaps of a figure adorning an earring or a bead on the body of a spider. Moche metalsmiths also developed the use of shell and stone inlay, and combinations of gold and silver, to maximize colour contrasts between gold, silver, orange-red shell or turquoise lapis lazuli.

Moche gilding also merits special mention. Instead of applying gold to the surface, bathing gold-alloy objects in natural acids depleted the outermost layer of silver or copper to leave a thin layer of pure gold – thus gilding from within.

LORD OF SIPÁN

The greatest single collection of Moche gold, silver and copper objects comes from 12 elite, unlooted burials at Sipán in the Lambayeque Valley. Spanning roughly 200 years from AD100 to 300, and including the burials of several lords and retainers, the tombs contained hundreds of gold, silver, copper, turquoise and shell objects and textiles.

Tomb I, of the Lord of Sipán (identified as the Warrior Priest of the Moche Sacrifice and Presentation ceremonies depicted in murals and on pottery), contained some 451 objects. His solid gold head crescent spanned 60cm (2ft). Gold and silver back-flaps lay beneath him. Above and below the body were textiles

adorned with gilded-copper platelets forming full-on human figures with turquoise bracelets, also a gilded-copper headdress with the same figure. His face is covered with a sheet-gold mask, his forehead with a gold strip, and gold, silver and copper nose-crescents and other jewellery adorn his face. He wears three pairs of gold and turquoise earspools (one depicts the lord himself, with a miniature detachable war club, swinging nosepiece and necklace), a gold and silver necklace of peanuts, and turquoise

Left: An exquisitely fine Moche gold and turquoise inlay 'supernatural' toucan, made of cut sheet gold, rolled, with repoussé, moulded and etched details, and revealing long-distance contacts between Pacific coast and tropical rainforest.

Above: The Sipán Lord 'royal' Moche tombs, among the few unlooted ancient Andean elite burials, produced prodigious amounts of gold and copper metalwork.

and gold bead bracelets. He holds gold and copper ingots and a gold rattle sceptre of war victims. Several gold and silver crescent-shaped bells depict the Decapitator.

OWL PRIEST

Tomb 2 contained the Owl Priest, wearing a gilded-copper headdress decorated with an owl with outspread wings, and a gilded-copper double necklace. Each strand comprised nine grimacing faces, the upper group with up-turned mouths, the lower group with down-turned mouths.

THE OLD LORD

Tomb 3 contained the body of the Old Lord of Sipán, buried 200 years earlier. He was buried with gold and silver sceptres and six necklaces (three gold and three silver). One of these was a necklace of 10 round gold beads depicting spiders perched on webs, a human face adorning each spider body. The delicate legs, webs, bodies and bead backing each required more than 100 solder points.

The Old Lord wore a gold nosepiece, and four gold and silver earspools. A miniature gold warrior (only centimetres/inches tall) holds a war club and round shield. His tiny nose-crescent moves, his turquoise eyes have tiny black stone pupils, and he wears a square-beaded turquoise necklace, turquoise earspools and a proportionately enormous thin, sheet-gold headdress of flaring bands and gold discs that dangle, plus a central owl.

Beneath the funerary mask of the Old Lord excavators found the astounding 'Ulluchu Man', at nearly 60cm (2ft) tall the opposite of the miniature warrior masterpiece. The sheet-metal figure was originally fixed to a textile banner, itself covered with gilded metal platelets and on which were found samples of ulluchu (papaya-like) fruit.

He is a human crab of gilded copper, with inlaid shell ornaments as eyes and on his abdomen and crab legs. He has a human face and legs, plus large, upheld

Below: A Moche moulded sheet-gold and gold and turquoise bead necklace worthy of a princess, probably representing the creator god Viracocha, or the founder Lord Naymlap.

crab claws and six crab legs. His headdress has curled ends and an owl face, plus a crescent *tumi*-knife-bladed top. He wears a necklace of round-eyed owl heads. Such imagery is associated with war prisoners and sacrifice, and the fruit may have contributed anticoagulant properties to the goblets of blood drunk in the Sacrifice and Presentation ceremony.

LOOTED TREASURES
Many more Moche gold, silver and alloy objects have been recovered. Sadly, most are known only out of context and identified as Moche by their style. For example, from the looted tombs of Loma

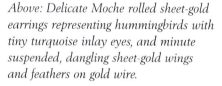

Above: Delicate Moche rolled sheet-gold earrings representing hummingbirds with tiny turquoise inlay eyes, and minute suspended, dangling sheet-gold wings and feathers on gold wire.

Negra in the Piura Valley come 14 hammered gold and silver nosepieces, pectorals and textile adornments. One is a simple, plain crescent. Others depict a face wearing a flaring crown; rows of crawling spiders; a row of seabirds; a double-headed, braided snake; facing crayfish; facing iguanas; the Decapitator holding a *tumi* knife and a severed head by the hair; a row of snails; and a row of alternating snake heads and human skulls.

Such rich finds display the gamut of Moche imagery: human sacrifice and religious ceremony, closeness to the sea, and long-distant trade (for the inlaid stones).

A fine example of the continuing illegal trade in precious antiquities is the recovery in London in 2006 of a large sheet-gold mask of the Moche Decapitator, presumed to have been looted 20 years ago from a tomb. The god's grimacing, fanged face is surrounded by curling head rays, intricately cut out with triangular, denticulate edges and ending in stylized, round-eyed creatures – the very image of the Decapitator so vividly depicted on the walls of Moche Huaca de la Luna in the Lambayeque Valley.

SICÁN LORDS AND METALSMITHS

The succeeding Sicán culture of the late Middle Horizon and first half of the Late Intermediate Period in the Lambayeque Valley has produced equally rich burials at Batán Grande. One grave of a lesser individual had more than 100kg (220lb) of copper alloy objects; richer graves held hundreds of gold and silver ornaments and vessels. Analyses of more than 1,000 artefacts has shown them to be 12- to 18-carat gold-silver-copper alloy – about the same as much gold jewellery made today. Other pieces, and most of the waste scrap metal, are tumbaga – a gold-silver-copper alloy of less than 10 carats.

MORE LOOTED TREASURES
Sadly, between the 1930s and 1970s the Lambayeque and adjacent valleys of the now Poma National Historical Sanctuary were desecrated by looters. Generations of *huaqueros* excavated more than

100,000 pits, seeking ancient tombs and their precious artefacts to satisfy the demands of greedy collectors. Thousands of objects have been purchased and thus saved by museums for the enjoyment of all, but the evidence of their cultural contexts has been destroyed.

TREASURE IN THE TOMB
The Sicán Lord in Tomb I in the Huaca Loro temple mound, dated *c*.1000AD, contained a man about 40–50 years old, entombed seated, his body inverted, and his head turned 180 degrees to be right-side up. He wore a gold mask (46 × 29cm/*c*.18 × 12in) and his body was painted deep red with cinnabar (mercuric sulphide), possibly to represent blood. His burial was accompanied by the sacrifices of two women and two children.

His *c*.9sq m (96sq ft) grave at the bottom of an 11m (36ft) shaft contained 1.2 tons (tonnes) of gold, silver and alloy objects arranged around him and in caches and containers.

His cloth mantle (now decayed away), placed beneath his body, was sewn with nearly 2,000 gold foil squares. Objects immediately around or on him included a wooden staff with gold decoration, a gold *tumi* knife, a gold headdress, gold

Above: An elite necklace of rolled and moulded sheet gold and moulded gold beads representing a Sicán Lord or possibly Viracocha the creator god.

shin covers, some tumbaga gloves measuring 2m (6½ ft) long, (one grasping a gold *kero* cup with a silver rattle base), and gold earspools. He was covered in a thick layer of stone, amber, shell and metal beads. Near by were *c*.500kg (*c*.1,100lb) of tumbaga scraps and *c*.250kg (*c*.550lb) of copper-arsenic tools.

There were caches of objects in niches dug into the tomb walls. A box lined with woven mats contained 60 objects, including 5 gold and silver crowns, 4 headbands, 12 *tumi*-knife-shaped head pieces, 6 head ornaments set with delicate gold feathers, three 3 fans, 14 discs (staff attachments or headdress backings), and 4 parabolic headpiece attachments.

One niche contained 1,500 bundles of small, uniformly sized *naipes* (copper-arsenic I-shaped bars – each bundle containing 12 or 13 pieces), which were possibly a form of 'currency'. Also two silver-alloy *tumi* knives, thousands of gold foil squares and up to 24 tumbaga miniature masks identical to the one worn by the lord.

Below: An elite Sicán burial skull adorned with a cloth headdress topped with feathers and rows of attached gold discs.

A LORDLY VISAGE

One tall head ornament comprised a gilded copper mask, painted red, and decorated with the face of the Sicán Lord, including inset precious stones. The forehead panel features a protruding vampire bat face and the tall crescent above it has etched geometric shapes, bulbous gold discs and an array of delicate golden feathers. There were several other similar pieces, the masks painted green or white.

The Sicán Lord image occurs on hundreds of objects, as a full figure or head only. He has a definitive half-circle face (the upper circle half being a crescent headdress) and eyes shaped like horizontal commas. His full figure often holds staffs. One Sicán grave contained more than 200 gold beakers with his image.

THE SICÁN METAL INDUSTRY

These objects come from the workshops of specialists. The placement even of the leftover scraps and inferior objects in tombs reveals their value, and emphasizes the prestige of the elite occupant.

Right: A Lambayeque-Sicán ceremonial bronze tumi *knife, topped with the delicate gold figure of a Sicán Lord or the Decapitator God, wearing a sun-flare or wave motif headdress.*

Batán Grande included mounds (the north platform of Huaca Loro and the north-east platform of Huaca Las Ventanas) supporting complexes of multi-roomed adobe buildings. They have split-level floors and integral adobe benches along their walls. In them excavators found copper slag and droplets of copper alloys from melting metal ore in bowl furnaces, no doubt using the locally abundant algarrobo (carob) trees as charcoal fuel.

Sicán-Lambayeque metalsmiths also ushered in the 'bronze age' of northern Peru. While gold-alloyed pieces advertise the social prestige of the owner, Sicán discovery and extensive use of arsenical-copper for making bronze enabled them to make sturdier blades and tools, the use of which was perpetuated by the Chimú and Incas after them.

Moreover, objects found in the Sicán Lord's caches reveal the existence of sophisticated metalworking training. Some of these pieces are of inferior quality and workmanship, as if made by lesser-skilled smiths or as practice pieces. The various stages of preparing the alloys, making the sheet metal, inscribing designs and cutting them out, and the artistry of forming and bonding the sheets, and producing

Left: Continuing the Moche tradition of fine sheet-gold work, Lambayeque-Sicán metalsmiths applied their skills to utilitarian objects such as this embossed copper-gold alloy kero *drinking cup, probably used for rituals.*

repoussé decorations and fine finishing, could be designated to apprentices and more skilled craftsmen as the work proceeded. For example, one gold cup with a Sicán Lord face has a raggedly chiselled chin, its silver base is pitted and traces of silver on the cup indicate that the silver was overheated and melted during bonding.

CHIMÚ AND INCA METALWORK

The spectacular Sipán and Batán Grande finds help to place ancient Andean metalwork into context and reveal details of metalworking techniques and 'industrial' output. Elite members of society, in control of the redistribution of wealth, dominated production and use. Spanish chronicles record thriving metallurgical industries in the Late Intermediate Kingdom of Chimú and among the Incas. The Incas forcibly resettled whole communities of metalsmiths in Cuzco to produce thousands of gold and silver objects in dedicated workshops.

MOCHE–SICÁN INHERITANCE

The Chimú subsumed and continued Sicán-Lambayeque smithing traditions, and much of their production is almost indistinguishable. They continued the Lambayeque introduction of making metal copies of ceramic shapes, particularly stirrup-spout bottles. Moche-Lambayeque fine metalwork traditions are exemplified by a Chimú silver stirrup-spout bottle and a pair of golden earspools, both with delicate repoussé decoration.

Below: A fine Chimú rolled sheet-gold, cone-shaped and turquoise bead necklace with gold face bead.

The Chimú silver stirrup-spout bottle is a miniature *audiencia* compound, part of a Chan Chan *ciudadela*. The curiously shaped piece is more like a sealed box surmounted by a stirrup spout. Intricately folded tiny sheet-silver figures decorate the bevelled ends of the bottle: an important official sits in a niche, while attendants stand at the vessel's corners. The flat sides and lower ends are decorated in repoussé, showing designs almost identical to those on the mud-sculpted walls of Chan Chan *ciudadelas*.

The surfaces of the pair of gold-silver Chimú earspools are covered in a story-like vignette in repoussé. At the tops are curious balconied structures, each surmounted by two tiny birds. Below the structure, a crinkled surface represents the sea, within which floats a rectangular raft. Two men on the raft stand back to back and bend over to receive spiny oyster shells from divers. Other divers collect more shells from the seabed. This charming picture must have made these earspools the pride and joy of some Chimú lord or lady!

INCA METALWORKING

Central highland cultures also had long-standing metalworking traditions. Some of the earliest copper working is from the Altiplano. Tiwanaku and Wari metalworkers produced distinctive styles in sheet metals, and their traditions were inherited by the Incas. Innovatively, Tiwanaku architects secured stone blocks with bronze staple-shaped clamps.

Two superlative examples exemplify Middle Horizon metallurgy. A Tiwanaku plaque of hammered sheet gold depicts a block-like face reminiscent of their stone sculptures. The hollowed eyes and mouth probably held stone insets. Fine incised lines around the face mimic the angular patterns of Tiwanaku textiles.

Above: This cast silver Inca male figurine represents an idealized Inca noble, identifiable by earlobes stretched from wearing ear discs. Note inlay gold bands on the hat, face and ankles, and inlay purple stone and orange-pink shell plaques.

A hammered sheet-silver Wari figure represents a warrior. The square-bodied, square-headed fighter wears a four-cornered hat, carries a shield and spear-thrower, and, like the Tiwanaku piece, is incised with fine lines representing his cloth tunic. He was one of a pair, the other being of gold, in characteristic Andean duality.

The great bulk of Inca gold and silver work was destroyed by the Spaniards. The chronicles report that they carried off and melted down 700 loads of gold sheathing from the Coricancha walls! The famous Cuzco garden of life-sized gold and silver plants and animals can only be imagined from remnant examples, such as a gold and silver maize stalk.

Other Inca gold and silver work has been found in provincial and mountaintop *capacocha* burials undiscovered by the Spaniards, such as votive llama figurines and cast-silver human figures. The Incas were fond of pairs of figures in gold and silver. Fortunately, many such figurines have survived, depicting males and females typically holding their hands to their breasts.

Below: Chimú lords, kings and priests used rolled and beaten sheet-gold gauntlets such as these, intricately decorated with embossed patterns and figures of lords or gods, probably in rituals and/or burials.

THE FIRST LOOTERS

Although the Incas honoured the Chan Chan *ciudadela* burial compounds of the Chimú dynasty, after the Spanish Conquest, they were systematically looted by the Spaniards, whose Castilian king established a royal smelter in the Moche valley to insure receipt of the crown's 20 per cent tax.

And there is the sad story of Atahualpa's ransom. Imprisoned in a palace room after his capture by Pizarro, Atahualpa realized that Spanish regard for gold and silver was different from Inca perceptions. He offered to fill his 5 x 6.75m (17 x 22ft) prison room with gold as high as he could reach. Pizarro, exploiting his advantage, also demanded that an adjoining small room be filled twice with silver. Atahualpa agreed, asked for two months for the task, and ordered the collection of gold and silver objects from all over the empire.

This singular episode highlights the different Andean and European perceptions of wealth. As religious symbols, Andean

Above: In conspicuous displays of wealth and power, Chimú and Inca nobles wore ceremonial tunics of fine alpaca wool with thousands of sheet-gold plaques or discs sewn onto them. This Inca example from southern Peru probably formed part of a mummy bundle.

gold and silver represented the essence of the sun and moon, but individual objects could be replaced. Their importance lay in the prestige they brought and in the imagery of the gods they displayed. Spanish interest was purely monetary. They cared neither for the artistry nor for any religious value the pieces held. In Spanish eyes, Inca gold and silver meant wealth and the destruction of idolatrous images.

This sad legacy continues. The unlooted tombs at Sipán and Batán Grande are rare examples of ancient Andean conspicuous consumption of precious metals in their social and ritual contexts.

CARVING AND BUILDING IN WOOD

Wood is rarely preserved in archaeological sites, except under special conditions. Enough has survived from Andean sites, however, to show that it was used in a variety of ways.

PRECERAMIC AND INITIAL PERIOD USES

Early migrants into the New World used wood for spear shafts and *atl-atl* spear-throwers (for big game), and throwing sticks (for small game), and also for stone-tool handles, digging sticks, mortars and fire drills, and for butchering, food collecting and processing.

Below: An Inca wooden coca snuff scoop, with a hand-forearm handle holding a disc scoop intricately carved with mythological figures, presumably representing drug-induced transformation.

Wooden earplugs are known from Preceramic sites. Burial offerings at the Initial Period coastal site of Ancón included a wooden bowl containing feathers, set beneath the head, and a tropical forest *chonta* wood figurine with inlaid shell eyes and articulated arms from a female burial. At Moxeke, a wooden figurine was found in one of the Huaca A platform rooms.

SNUFF TABLETS AND *KEROS*

Tiwanaku and Wari shamans used flat wooden snuff tablets for preparing coca and other hallucinogenic substances. Carved and highly polished, their handles depict animals, beast-headed men and geometric designs, inlaid with stone ornament. Other portable wooden artefacts depicted the Staff Deity.

Elaborately carved wooden *kero* drinking cups were a Middle Horizon speciality, continued by the Incas and into Spanish Colonial times. Many are painted. One carved Tiwanaku example depicts the Staff Deity dressed almost identically to the central figure on the Gateway of the Sun at the Kalasasaya compound.

An exquisite Chimú wooden *kero* comprises a cup, painted with a simple red and black design and black rim, on top of which was a carved figure inlaid with gold, turquoise and shell, standing on a mushroom-shaped pedestal. The grinning figure has a row of rectangular shell teeth, round, red shell eyes and a pillbox hat with shell-inlaid earflaps, and holds a golden cross at chest height.

WOODEN LITTERS

The celebrated Lambayeque-Chimú ceremonial litter is an elaborate frame sheathed with sheet gold. Six main panels and two smaller ones represent small 'houses'. The main houses have central doorways, sloping roofs and dangling gold crescent-shaped eave decorations. Inside stand three Sicán Lord warriors, with characteristic horizontal-comma eyes.

Above: A carved wooden post showing a stylized face, probably part of a thatched roof support, demonstrates Inca carving skill.

Single figures stand in the end houses and between the upper row of houses. Holes indicate that the litter was originally studded with feathers. Such a rich item must have transported a ruler.

The frame of a carved wooden litter was also found in the Lord Sicán tomb at Batán Grande.

IDOLS AND COFFINS

A small, windowless temple atop the main platform at the pilgrimage city of Pachacamac housed a carved wooden idol. It was kept behind a veil, and only priests were allowed to ascend the platform and enter the temple. The figure was carved with human faces on both sides, to represent duality. This idol was destroyed by Hernando Pizarro, whereupon the oracle 'fell silent', but several similar figures, presumed from Pachacamac, are in museums.

Above: Kero *drinking cups were for everyday use and for ritual drinking. Made of wood, pottery and precious metals, this Inca wooden example, depicting an Inca warrior, was probably used by a noble.*

The entryways of Chimú royal *ciudadelas* at Chan Chan were guarded by carved wooden figures standing in niches.

The Chachapoyas stood a row of upright wooden coffins on a rocky ledge at Karajia, on the north-western Inca tropical mountain borders. The 'heads' are carved with full, round beards and wear cylindrical hats, some with human skulls on top. The bodies are painted as clothing. At Los Pinchudos, they built round burial structures with stone mosaic exteriors, above which they placed rows of wooden, highly phallic male figures.

The Moche Sipán Lord was laid to rest on a wooden-slat support and placed in a wooden plank coffin, sewn with cords.

WOOD IN ARCHITECTURE

Rafters of wood supported the thatch roofs of stone and adobe walls. Highland and tropical wood was imported to coastal and desert areas for this purpose, and many adobe walls have insets for beams (for example at Sipán).

Wood began to be imported in the late Preceramic Period. Wooden thresholds at coastal Río Seco are made from trees that grow at 1,450–3,000m (4,785–10,000ft). The importance of these exchange links is revealed by the fact that neither wood nor highland obsidian was essential in the coastal economy, yet they were sought in preference to local materials. At Initial Period Garagay, wooden posts set into lined circular pits supported the roof of the Middle Temple.

The Chimú used wooden moulds to decorate their Late Intermediate Period mud walls.

COMMON TOOLS

A number of Late Intermediate Period Chancay wooden burial masks were found in non-elite graves. With basic features, shell inlays for eyes and often painted red, they appear to be a widespread extension of ancestor cults among citizens.

The Ica-Chincha and other central Peruvian coastal peoples made long, paddle-like objects with delicately carved openwork on the paddle top and along the shaft. One example has a row of long-beaked seabirds and a larger seabird on top of the shaft 'pommel'. Such artefacts are variously identified as ceremonial digging sticks, boat paddles or raft-steering paddles.

Balsa-wood rafts were the standard coastal trading vessels, such as the raft encountered by Pizarro's captain, Bartholomew Ruíz, in 1527 on his second voyage down the north-west South American coast. Laden with Inca gold and silver objects and textiles, the traders were from the Inca port of Tumbes.

Wood was essential in textile weaving for weaving tools and parts. Spindle whorls were ceramic or wood. Backstrap looms required wooden warp beams, shed sticks, heddle rods, bobbins and beating paddles.

Humblest of all, farmers' digging and planting sticks, and handles for agricultural implements, were essential items in planting, tending and harvesting the produce of villages, towns, city-states, kingdoms and empires throughout ancient Andean history.

Below: One of the finest surviving pieces of ancient Andean woodwork is this Lambayeque-Chimú royal litter or palanquin.

STONE, SHELL AND BONE

Ancient Andeans used semi-precious stones, bone and shell for small items of jewellery, on their own or as inlaid work.

OBSIDIAN
The earliest Andean hunter-gatherers used local stone for tools. Obsidian (natural volcanic glass), only available from specific highland locations, soon became preferred and was imported by coastal fishing and farming villages from Preceramic times.

TURQUOISE AND LAPIS LAZULI
Sources of turquoise and lapis lazuli (lazurite) were also rare – turquoise coming from the highlands, lapis lazuli

Below: A Chimú wooden bowl, with inlaid mother-of-pearl, turquoise and spondylus shell representing a wide-eyed sun-god-like face-skull.

from northern Chile. Tiny lapis lazuli beads were found in the hand of the highland Waywaka burial, which also contained the earliest gold foil, *c.*1500BC. Cupisnique burials include shell, turquoise, lapis lazuli and quartz crystal necklaces, and Chavín craftsmen also used exotic stones.

Moche jewellers used stone appliqué extensively, especially finely shaped turquoise chips. Sicán-Lambayeque craftsmen introduced techniques of inlaying shaped and polished turquoise and shell in gold and silver work, and in wood.

One of three gold and turquoise earspools in the Moche Sipán Lord's tomb depicts the lord himself, with two attendants flanking him. All three figures wear headdresses made up of minute turquoise chips. Another earspool has a running

Above: A shell container for lime, used with coca-leaf chewing, whose shape the artisan used to form into a stylized bird, from the Capuli culture of Ecuador.

deer made of shaped turquoise chips and tiny dark stone cloven hoofs, within a gold-bead and turquoise-chip circle.

Wari and Tiwanaku royalty imported turquoise, lapis lazuli, chrysacola minerals and greenstones from distant sources. An elaborate wooden Tiwanaku *kero* cup comprises a cup and 'stem' in the shape of a figure holding a gold cross. His clothing has numerous shell and gold inlays and a turquoise stone in the middle of the headdress. Forty intricately carved, 25mm (1in) figurines of tiny stone and shell chips and gold foil were found at Wari Pikillacta.

The body of the Sicán Lord at Batán Grande was covered in a 10cm- (4in-) thick layer of amber, shell, gold and silver alloy and stone beads (sodalite, amethyst, quartz crystal, turquoise, fluorite and calcite).

Emeralds were imported from Colombia. They were inlaid in Sicán-Lambayeque, Chimú and Inca jewellery.

Quartz crystals were especially coveted by shamans for ritual divinations.

SHELL
Jewellery was made from Preceramic times, mostly as shell necklaces. Shells were abundant at Preceramic coastal villages, and they were exchanged for wood and obsidian with people in the highland regions.

Strombus (conch) and spondylus (thorny oyster; *Spondylus princeps*) shells were especially sought. Shell trumpets were used in religious ritual. One sculptured figure in Chavín de Huántar's circular sunken court, for example, blows a conch trumpet. The dynastic founder Naymlap's royal entourage included Fonga Sigde, 'Blower of the Shell Trumpet', and Pitz Zofi 'Preparer of the Way', who ground and spread shell dust before his ruler.

Spondylus shells were particularly prestigious. They are found only in the warmer waters off the Ecuadorian coast and farther north, and therefore are exotic imports. Preceramic and Initial Period coastal peoples imported them, and Cupisnique people made thousands of shell beads and pendants from local shells and spondylus. They sewed shells to their garments and even made bead skirts.

In the Early Horizon, as well as at Chavín de Huántar and other highland sites, spondylus shells were traded as far south as Paracas in southern coastal Peru. Elite individuals in rich mummy bundle burials wear necklaces of tubular and spondylus shells, thus declaring their high social status.

Sicán-Lambayeque lords and Chimú kings imported thousands of spondylus shells for their craftsmen to shape into jewellery and inlay in gold objects. Fonga Sigde was responsible for importing spondylus shells to Naymlap's court and may have worn earplugs such as the gold pair depicting divers collecting spondylus shells and handing them to men on rafts. Thorny oysters are even depicted and sculpted on Chimú ceramics and sculpted mud walls.

A particularly fine Chimú spondylus shell piece exemplifies the quality of their craftsmanship. Having removed the spines and smoothed the edge of an orange spondylus, the jeweller inlaid dark purple *Spondylus calcifer* into the top portion, to frame two exquisite, darker orange *S. princeps* birds and diamonds. Facing each other in characteristic, symbolic Andean duality, each bird pecks a fish, a typical Chimú motif. The birds and fish have tiny inlaid turquoise eyes, and the whole is highly finished to a uniform smoothness.

Inca craftsmen (or Chimú craftsmen resettled in Cuzco) also worked spondylus. For example, an especially fine necklace of 13 rectangular spondylus plaques was found on the Inca *capacocha* burial of a boy at Llullaillaco. Chachapoyas people included spondylus shell offerings in their round, stone mosaic burial structures.

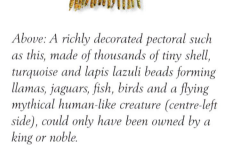

Above: A richly decorated pectoral such as this, made of thousands of tiny shell, turquoise and lapis lazuli beads forming llamas, jaguars, fish, birds and a flying mythical human-like creature (centre-left side), could only have been owned by a king or noble.

CARVING IN BONE

Bone was also carved from early times. There are bone pins inlaid with turquoise from La Galgada burials, and an amber pendant. Four bone figurines with round staring eyes were found at Cerro Narrio in southern Ecuador.

Carved Chavín pieces include a human finger bone with incised bird motifs, found in the gallery above the Lanzón Stela, a hallucinogenic snuff spatula incised with a snarling feline motif (with traces of red paint) and two carved objects from Shillacoto (rubbed with charcoal).

A pair of highly polished, naked whalebone figurines from a Nazca grave have square shell headdresses and painted eyes.

A Moche bone spatula is carved as a clenched fist and forearm, incised with intertwined figures and inlaid with turquoise chips.

Incas soldiers used skulls of enemy slain as gruesome victory cups from which to drink *chicha* beer!

Below: These five finely carved bone figurines of the Early Intermediate Period Narrio culture of Ecuador might have had shell or stone inlay eyes and were probably temple pieces, possibly fertility figurines.

FUNERARY ART

Ancient Andean production of ceramics, textiles, metal objects and metal, stone, shell and bone jewellery served multiple purposes. Andean 'art' was not produced for its own sake. Craftsmanship, artistry and aesthetic aspects were important, but the two primary purposes for its production were religious and economic.

POWER, CONTROL AND ARTISTRY

High-quality craftsmanship and artistry were important in producing sumptuary items, to enable individuals of high social status to advertise and emphasize their position. As with other aspects of Andean civilization, much was aimed at demonstrating power and control, and with impressing others with these issues. Much had to do with essence. Dressing in the most elaborate and exquisite garments, wearing the best jewellery and using the best-quality pottery were outward signs that the person wearing and using these items was also of superior quality.

Although the craftsmen and those people for whom the objects were produced cannot have been oblivious to the pure aesthetics of the pieces, they were striving to represent a mindset constantly influenced by religious considerations.

Below: Elite burial masks are thought to represent transformation of the deceased into a deity. This late Moche or Lambayeque gold example represents another 'transformation' and the concept of 'essence', as the gold bears traces of covering paint!

The social evolution of Andean civilization produced a class of citizens – royalty, nobility and religious leaders – whose purpose was to rule, administer the economy and intervene with the gods on the public's behalf. The entire worldview was governed by the need to maintain balance with divine powers for the welfare of humans and their life on Earth.

RELIGIOUS SYMBOLISM AND ECONOMIC BALANCE

Production of luxury items was to honour the deities and to provide for the redistribution of wealth, however unequally, within Andean society. The deposition of so much sumptuary production in royal and elite graves reveals that the value of the precious metals and other high-quality objects came not from their financial value, but

Above: The earliest funerary 'art' is represented in Chinchorros burials (northern Chile from c.6000BC), in which bodies were preserved with salt after removing the viscera and stuffing with straw, then shaped in clay and given facial features.

from their worth as demonstrations of power, control, rank and an ability to consume conspicuously. Placing such tremendous wealth in tombs effectively removed it from circulation among humans, but it enhanced the prestige of the tomb's occupant and secured favour from the gods.

Death in the ancient Andean world was only the end of one stage in a cycle of being. Entombment was not necessarily permanent. In many cultures, the mummies (Inca *mallquis*) were regularly 'worshipped', kept in accessible tombs, or in special caves or temples, and brought out on ritual occasions to be consulted,

Above: The burial of an Inca noble, possibly a southern lord, as the text is Aymara of the Titicaca region and the mummy is being placed in a stone chullpa *tower in which an earlier skeleton sits (depicted in Poma de Ayala's* Nueva Corónica, c.1615).

entertained and given food and drink. Nazca tombs and *chullpa* burial towers were kinship mausoleums regularly reopened for the deposit of descendants through generations.

The removal of luxury goods from circulation also perpetuated the need for their production and supported continued elite conspicuous consumption, and therefore royal, elite and religious control. The effect was to keep the economy active and healthy. The bulk of the population, engaged in agriculture, supported elite and religious leaders, and the craftspeople necessary to produce sumptuary goods. The exclusivity of Chimú royal compounds at Chan Chan and their massive storage rooms are exemplary in this regard.

The situation can be regarded as an unconscious perpetuation of the Andean cyclical worldview.

CONFIRMING CEREMONY

Funerary art brings together all forms of Andean craft production. Although much of what has been found in burials and tombs was probably worn and used in life, it was also ultimately made in preparation for burial. Religious symbolism was paramount, both in the subject matter portrayed on the objects and in its presentation in the tombs.

Confirmation of the religious rituals depicted on Moche murals, for example, has been found in the Sipán and other elite burials. The principal bodies were dressed in identical regalia to that worn by the priests and priestesses of Moche Sacrifice and Presentation ceremonies shown on walls and ceramics. Their attendants in the tombs were their retainers for the next state of being, and were sacrificial victims, part of Andean religious practice from the earliest Initial Period tombs at U-shaped ceremonial centres.

In Sicán-Lambayeque elite burials at Batán Grande one tomb contained 17 sacrificial victims. And the caches of copper *naipes* suggest both that Batán Grande was the centre for their production and that their value was not only an exchange mechanism in life.

JUST FOR BURIAL

The preparation of items specifically for burial is suggested by Paracas and Nazca mummy bundles. Some of the textiles, whose intricate weaving and complex symbolism necessitated great labour over long time periods (sometimes perhaps even a lifetime), are unfinished. This indicates that the individual died before the item could be finished by the maker. Other possible explanations are that the items were being made expressly for the eventuality of burial with the deceased, but that it was also necessary to include them unfinished because they 'belonged' to that person in every sense. Alternatively, some items might have been deliberately left unfinished so that they could be completed by the individual in the next life.

The concept that a set of possessions was specific to an individual may also be the explanation of the deposition of inferior goods in the Sicán Lord's tomb. All items made for and possessed by that person were part of his being and therefore were necessary for his or her completeness on 'the other side', in the next state of being.

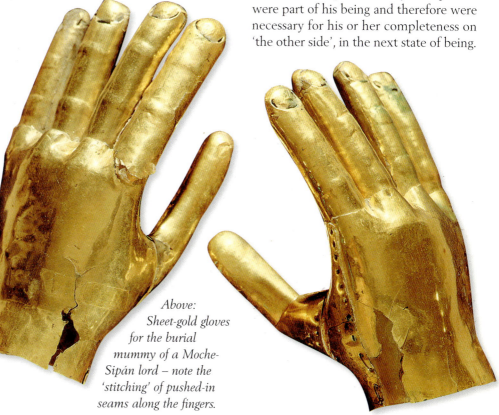

Above: Sheet-gold gloves for the burial mummy of a Moche-Sipán lord – note the 'stitching' of pushed-in seams along the fingers.

GLOSSARY

aclla (or acllyacona) a chosen woman, selected to serve in the imperial cult of Inti
adobe mud brick
Altiplano high plateaux regions, especially in southern Andes
amaru mythical serpent-dragon figure
amautas Inca court officials
apo Inca official in charge of a *suyu*
apu type of *huaca* – sacred mountain deity
atl-atl spear-thrower used by hunter-gatherers and in warfare
Auca Runa people of the fourth age in Inca creation
ayar legendary Inca ancestor
aylloscas Inca gambling game played by nobles
ayllu community bound in kinship both by blood and marriage, and with territory held in common
Aymara principal Inca language of the south Andes
ayni Aymara term for *mit'a*
capacocha specially selected Inca sacrificial victim, usually noble, often a child
cayman South American freshwater alligator
ceque sacred pathway or sight line in Andean religion, especially from Inca Cuzco.

chachapuma puma-headed person/statuary
charqui strips of sun-dried and freeze-dried meat or fish
chasqui Inca imperial messenger/road runner
chicha beer made from fermented maize
chullpa Late Intermediate Period and Late Horizon stone burial towers
ciudadela huge walled compound of ruling or dead Chimú king at Chan Chan
collcas Inca state storehouses for large quantities of such staples as *charqui* and *chuño*
coya official wife of the Inca emperor
curacas local leader or chief, or one of several levels of Inca officials
geoglyph geometric shape or figure from the Nazca Desert and other Andean Area places
hanan upper: applied to one *moiety* of a lineage group (*ayllu*) and to a subdivision of a town or province
Hanan Pacha the Inca world of above
huaca sacred place
hurin lower: applied to one *moiety* of a lineage group (*ayllu*) and to a subdivision of a town or province
Inti the sun god; also the Inca emperor
intihuatana 'hitching post of the sun' – Inca rock platform used as a sort of altar for sun observation and worship
Kai Pacha the Inca world of the living
kallanka large rectangular Inca hall used for public purposes
kancha walled enclosure of residential and storage buildings
kero Andean drinking cup

mallquis mummified remains of Inca rulers and nobility
mama female part of the Early Horizon Yaya-Mama cult around Lake Titicaca
manioc low-altitude tropical vegetable tuber
mashwa low-altitude Andean vegetable tuber
mit'a 'tax' obligation to do periodic labour for the state
mitimaes peoples redistributed within the Inca Empire
moiety half division of a lineage group (e.g. *ayllus*). The two intermarriageable family groups of a descent lineage
montaña the forested slopes of the eastern Andes
oca high-altitude Andean vegetable tuber
pacarina a place of origin
pachacuti turning over, revolution, a cycle of world events or states of being
pampas extensive temperate, upland grasslands in the south Andean Area
panacas Cuzco imperial *ayllus* comprising the descendants of each Inca emperor
plazas hundidas 'hidden' open courts, semi-subterranean
pukarás Late Intermediate and Late Horizon hilltop fortresses
puna Andean sierra basin or valley, a high, cold plateau
Purun Runa people of the third age in Inca creation
Quechua principal Inca language of the central and northern Andes
quincha mud-plastered cane used in Andean house walls
quinoa high-protein grain
quipus Inca system of knotting wool and cotton strings to record basic economic and historical information

Sapa the Inca emperor
sinchis warrior leaders of the Later Intermediate Period and Late Horizon who built hilltop fortifications called *pukarás*
stela carved stone ritual monument or statuary
suyu division of the Inca Empire, which comprised four *suyus*, or 'quarters', of unequal size
Tahuantinsuyu 'The four parts' – Inca name for their empire
tambos way-stations on Inca, Wari and Tiwanaku roads
tarwi high-protein grain
tumbaga amalgamation of copper and gold (or sometimes silver)
tumi copper or bronze crescent-shaped knife used for ritual decapitation; ceremonial *tumis* were made of precious metals
tupu large copper pin used by Inca women to secure a mantle. Nobles used *tupus* of precious metals
Uku Pacha the Inca world of below
ulluco Highland vegetable tuber
U-shaped complex Andean and coastal western valley temples comprising a main end platform mound with subsidiary long platform mounds extending from its front corners to form a U shape enclosing a plaza
Wari Runa people of the second age in Inca creation
Wari Wiracocharuna people of the first age in Inca creation
yaya male part of the Early Horizon Yaya-Mama Cult around Lake Titicaca
yuca high-altitude Andean vegetable tuber

INDEX